The Brain, Education, and the Competitive Edge

Geoffrey Caine
Renate Nummela Caine

The Scarecrow Press, Inc.
A Scarecrow Education Book
Lanham, Maryland, and London
2001

SCARECROW PRESS, INC.
A Scarecrow Education Book

Published in the United States of America
by Scarecrow Press, Inc.
4720 Boston Way, Lanham, Maryland 20706
www.scarecroweducation.com

4 Pleydell Gardens, Folkeston
Kent CT20 2DN, England

British Library Cataloguing-in-Publication Information Available

Library of Congress Cataloging-in-Publication Data

Caine, Geoffrey.
    The brain, education, and the competitive edge / Geoffrey Caine and Renate Nummela Caine.
        p. cm.—(A Scarecrow education book)
    Includes bibliographical references and index.
    ISBN 0-8108-4060-X (alk. paper)—ISBN 0-8108-4061-8 (pbk. : alk. paper)
        1. Educational change—United States. 2. Teaching—United States. 3. Experiential
    learning—United States. I. Caine, Renate Nummela. II. Title. III. Series
    LA210 .C284 2001
    370'.973—dc21

                                                                    2001031077

⊗™ The paper used in this publication meets the minimum requirements
of American National Standard for Information Sciences—Permanence of
Paper for Printed Library Materials, ANSI/NISO Z39.48-1992.
Manufactured in the United States of America.

Contents

Preface

Effective education is the foundation for effective living. Unfortunately, many countries and cultures are employing a late twentieth-century political process in an attempt to perfect an early twentieth-century model of schools, based on seventeenth-century beliefs about how people learn, in order to prepare children for the twenty-first century. The result is that most current education reform is heading in a direction that can not possibly succeed. We hope that this book provides some insight into a more useful direction.

Someone (we believe H. L. Mencken) once said that "for every complex problem there is a solution that is simple, neat, and wrong." The United States and many other countries are gripped by a deep concern about the quality of education. That is where the complex problem begins. The proposed solution that is sweeping almost all before it is to spell out higher standards, teach to those standards on a grade-by-grade and year-by-year basis, measure the results by standardized tests, and hold teachers and schools accountable on the basis of those test results. That is the wrong solution. In fact, the solution is part of the problem. While test scores will climb to some extent, particularly at the low end of the competency spectrum, overall real standards are likely to decline—perhaps precipitously.

There clearly is a convergence of competing forces tearing at the fabric of education. Public education is feared to be inadequate (as indicated, for instance by the perceived results of U.S. students on international tests) and unsafe (as revealed by the tragedies of students shooting students). Homeschooling is proliferating. Alternatives, ranging from charter schools to vouchers, are receiving serious attention. Meanwhile a potent combination of business and technology (Technobusiness) is seeking both to capitalize on the traditional system and to compete with it. And the entire situation is highly politicized.

Unfortunately, there is no consensus as to what really effective education looks like. Central to the dispute is the flood of recent research on how the brain/mind actually learns. The situation is difficult because almost all the educational reforms currently being advocated fail to consider what is now known about powerful learning.

In this book we examine many of the opposing forces and unpack the two competing approaches to learning, teaching, and education. The one we introduce above and which we call the standard model, aims at standardization of educational processes in the name of high standards. One of the ensuing paradoxes is that excessive standardization is known to undermine creativity, a source of vitality and a very great strength of countries such as the United States. The other approach— more powerful and more effective—is what we call the guided experience approach. We show that guided experience supplemented by direct instruction is perfectly aligned with the way that the brain was biologically designed to learn. We illustrate its efficacy with evidence of powerful learning in the everyday world, and show why performance assessment is so much more valuable than test scores. We also describe examples of superb education from around the world, ranging from early childhood education and powerful homeschooling to excellent secondary schooling.

The tragedy of educational reform in recent times is that the system itself is designed for the standard model, and so the guided-experience approach continuously founders on the reefs of bureaucracy, misinformation, and fear. At this turn of the millennium, however, emerging out of the uncertainty and turbulence are a number of trends which cumulatively suggest that, side by side with the push for standardization, is a massive reinvention of education. New configurations include: charter schools flourishing in many regions, and beginning to expand across district and state borders; parents pooling resources, using technology, and engaging in collective homeschooling; providers of distance education entering into partnerships with local government schools; entire virtual schools being created; systems of public education crossing traditional boundaries and working with business, parents, and others to function at much higher levels.

Our objective is to contribute to a substantial improvement in real standards. For that to happen, educators and the larger community need to return to the fundamentals that count. We need to see how and why the standard model of education arose. We need to grasp the biological basis of learning, and appreciate the essential differences between memorization and making sense of experience. We need to get a handle on the pervasive nature of learning from experience in every domain of human existence. We need to come to terms with the elements that make learning from experience work, and understand how to incorporate those elements into schooling. And with all of that as a foundation, those who care about high-level learning and leading-edge education need to pool resources and find natural partners. In addition to finding ways to work together we need to develop a common language and collectively spread a message and shed light upon the profoundly mistaken beliefs that currently prevail.

We argue that ultimately, the key to really effective education is to align the best of what is known about learning and teaching with systems that facilitate such learning and teaching, appropriately supported by the larger culture within which education occurs. The alignment may, but will not necessarily, occur in the United States. However there is absolutely no doubt that those communities that grasp and implement such an alignment will develop a vastly superior system of education, and in the medium to long term they will clearly have a significant competitive edge.

This book synthesizes work in which we have been engaged for many years. In our first book, *Making Connections: Teaching and the Human Brain* (1991) we developed a set of general principles of learning and some implications for education that have now found their way into every continent. Since then we have worked with many schools, districts, organizations, and businesses, both to test our ideas and to implement them. In the course of this work we have learned an enormous amount, and can not adequately thank all of those who have contributed to our understanding. Those wishing to track our path might like to read *Education on the Edge of Possibility* (1997) in which we describe our long-term work with two schools and our battle to grasp the complexities of systems in general.

Most of our writing has been for the education community. A major reason for writing this book is to share our observations and experiences with all those noneducators who are interested in and wish to improve education. We hope that these ideas and stories will assist them to evaluate proposals and programs and promises, formulate policies, test and assess products and services, campaign for better educational environments, ride the waves of change more safely, and generally participate more effectively in preparing the future for all our children.

We have been particularly gratified by the many encounters we have had with people engaged in similar ventures, and with the many opportunities to compare notes and share stories. Of specific importance in writing this book have been the feedback and comments of family, friends, and colleagues who were kind enough to read it. They include Nancy Brothers, Donald and Peggy Caine, Sam Crowell, Ronnie Durie, Jenny Flynn, Karl Klimek, Elsie Ritsenhein, Ken Thompson, and Cindy Tucker. More generally, we would like to thank the many superb educators, informed parents, and diligent researchers who have helped our understanding to grow. Thanks also to our dear friend John Marshall for the cartoons that set the stage for each chapter.

Geoffrey Caine
Renate Nummela Caine
Idyllwild, California, February 2001

CHAPTER 1

Education in the Eye of the Storm

Things fall apart, the center cannot hold. Mere anarchy is released upon the world. (W. B. Yeats, 1922)

My first priority—in fact my first, second and third priority—is education. (California Governor Davis, January 6, 1999)

[A] report on the childhoods of four hundred famous modern persons, states that three fifths of the subjects "had serious school problems": Rejection of the classroom is an international phenomenon and has little to do with whether the schools are public or private, secular or clerical, or with the philosophy of teaching employed in the various schools. (James Hillman, 1996, p. 101)

About 63 million years ago an asteroid is said to have collided with the earth. The impact was so great, and the devastation so extensive, that the dinosaurs (which had dominated life for the preceding 100 million years) soon became extinct. Public education is facing a similar predicament. Never has education been more important nor in so much confusion. Unfortunately, although there are some exceptional schools and processes, the waves of confusion are threatening to sink public education rather than improve it.

PUBLIC CONCERN

The dinosaurs (we can assume) were oblivious to their impending doom. In contrast, much of the public does have a sense that something is seriously wrong with education though specific concerns vary widely. The issue bubbles up continuously, and gets more urgent over time. Americans panicked about the quality of math and science education and the possible implications for national defense when Sputnik was launched by the Soviet Union in 1957. In the 1983 report, *A Nation at Risk*, one key finding was that

> Secondary school curricula have been homogenized, diluted, and diffused to the point that they no longer have a central purpose. In effect, we have a cafeteria style curriculum in which the appetizers and desserts can easily be mistaken for the main courses.

A major recommendation was that state and local high school graduation requirements be strengthened.

More recently a major, bipartisan call to arms in the United States was *The Goals 2000: Educate America Act* which "recognizes that education is a state and local responsibility, but it must also be a national priority." It supported states and communities in their efforts to improve academic achievement by raising academic standards, supporting high-quality teacher professional development, and increasing parental and community involvement in education (Department of Education home page: www.ed.gov/G2K/).

Poll after poll confirms that education has become the public's number one concern in the United States, and the issue featured prominently in the 2000 presidential campaign. Parents care about the future of their kids, and believe that a sound education matters. Social activists argue that a good education system is the lynchpin of democracy. Major figures in business have been sounding their alarm for years. Where, they say, can they find workers and managers with the qualities to function well in a changing and global economy? Are students creative, motivated, diligent, competent, mature, capable of change, and ready to learn and learn again? David Kearns, the then CEO of Xerox, undertook the task of presiding over the New American Schools Development Corporation, a nonprofit organization that launched a major competition in 1991 for replicable forms of innovative and more effective schools. Thousands of individuals, schools, and businesses were galvanized into action in the search for new types of schools that could benefit the public at large. Others have made substantial contributions. For example, in 1993 the Annenberg Foundation gave $500 million dollars to improve education in the United States, and in 1999, the Bill and Melinda Gates Foundation gave more than $100 million dollars in grants.

COMPETING INTERESTS

In fact education is rife with cross currents and waves of competing interests clashing with each other. The traditional system of public education is fighting for survival and respect while a potent combination of business and technology (which we call Technobusiness) is seeking both to capitalize on the traditional system and to compete with it. Added to these conflicting interests are the different voices of homeschoolers, some of whom want freedom to provide a strongly prescriptive religious upbringing for their children while others want equal freedom to provide their children with autonomy and choice in spiritual and social matters.

Contributing to the mix is a strong urge, driven in part by what leading organization consultant Margaret Wheatley calls the longing to belong, and in part by a desire to make sense of things and connect with something larger then we are—often based on very strong spiritual convictions. The peculiar result is that many factions and interest groups that once seemed to be at odds with each other sometimes seem to be speaking with a common voice. Thus, often to their mutual surprise, some professional educators and homeschooling parents are beginning to dialogue with each other.

Underlying much of this turbulence is an almost competitive blood lust with education at its core: competition for jobs, for power, for status, for money, for survival, for preeminence in a highly testosterone-charged world. Most of the struggle is taking place under intense media scrutiny. And the entire situation is highly politicized as campaigns for improving education and slogans about education issue forth from every party at every level of the political spectrum.

The bottom line is that there is a convergence of competing forces that are collectively tearing at the fabric of the system while there is no consensus as to what really effective education looks like. For kids and families this can be soul wrenching. For any business or government that genuinely thinks in the medium to long term, the questions should be equally profound, and disturbing.

LOWERING STANDARDS BY TRYING TO RAISE THEM

Let us begin with the familiar picture of a classroom, where a teacher is at the front and students are seated in rows before her. She knows the curriculum, devises lesson plans, and spends her time telling the students what they need to know or asking questions to which they need to respond. She will use a textbook, going through it chapter by chapter, and usually setting questions at the back as homework assignments. And, of course, students will also be tested periodically. We call this approach to schooling the "standard model," and describe it in detail in the next chapter.

The standard model is based on the notion that there is a core curriculum of facts and skills, specified by the state, that all students should master in roughly the same amount of time (say, 12 years). School is a place where teachers present or deliver those facts to students and train students on those skills. Every school in a district or state is organized in approximately the same way, based on gathering students into classes organized according to age and grade.

While there are different ways in which this model of schooling can be improved, the approach currently sweeping the United States and many other countries, often in the guise of revolutionizing education, is to raise the standards of the standard model by large-scale standardization. "Raising standards" tends to mean adding more and more to the prescribed curriculum; "improving teaching" tends to mean ensuring that more and more teachers follow a prescribed methodology; and "holding teachers and schools accountable" tends to mean allocating rewards or punishments according to how well students do on standardized tests. In the rest of this book we will refer to this approach as "standardization."

Standardization is perfectly understandable. In times of immense uncertainty, when results need to be improved, the overwhelming temptation is to take more and more control of what is happening. Unfortunately, standardization is an inadequate and possibly disastrous response, and most of the battles being fought over public education are the wrong battles. In that respect educational combatants are much like the dinosaurs, fighting viciously for supremacy in a world that is about to make most of the struggle irrelevant.

A Curious Paradox

The confusing nature of the problem is not immediately obvious, but it can be discerned when we dig beneath the surface of attempts at educational reform and discover a curious paradox. The efforts to improve public education by standardization is leading to the eradication of many exceptional practices, and downskilling many exceptional people who demonstrably function at a much higher level than the norm. Standardization, therefore, is clearly lowering standards in some ways. Here, by way of example, is a true story, though names and dates have been changed.

Megan Burrows is one of the best teachers we have ever encountered. Her standards, we should add, were high according to orthodox measures. When we began working with her school its reading scores were second lowest in the district. Five years later, the scores overall were second highest. Megan, with her partner Rhonda, accounted for a substantial part of that increase.

Their story, however, becomes rather bizarre. The two had become so good that the district had asked for their assistance in the training and inservice of other teachers. Many teachers from nearby schools were invited to spend several hours in the classrooms run by the two in order to see excellence at work. By teaching in the sophisticated way that they were, very young children were learning to read, becoming proficient at math, and also acquiring some genuine thinking skills and a degree of self-control. Yet at precisely the same time as the district was calling upon their expertise to help others, the district began implementing state mandated programs that required that every teacher, Rhonda and Megan included, start incorporating prescribed texts and mandated reading and writing practices into their daily routines at prescribed times, irrespective of the results that had been achieved and of the impact on and disruption of the elegant, free flowing, and highly demanding learning environments that the two teachers had been developing.

Megan and Rhonda are foot soldiers in an education system at war with itself. The story is one of many. It shows that, in the name of educational excellence, a quite peculiar pattern is developing in many parts of public education as a consequence of the standardization movement.

Clear concern is being expressed for improved performance and higher standards. Greater coverage of subject areas is being specified, and additional standards are being established, at national, state, district, and subject matter levels.

Success depends on student performance on high-stakes tests, many of which are highly standardized. Most of the tests are statewide and operate at prescribed grade levels. Results are explored and displayed in the media, and comparisons are made between grades, schools, districts, states, and nations.

Schools and personnel are accountable for the results of their students on these tests. The lowest performing schools are identified in a variety of ways, and they can have funding reduced, be taken over, or be penalized in other ways. Teachers are also being put under the spotlight, with rewards—usually financial—being offered for those who produce good results, and penalties being sought for those whose students underperform.

In order to raise standards, methods of teaching are becoming highly standardized. Within public education systems, many teacher practices are being mandated to the point where less and less room is available for professional and independent decisions to be made. In fact professionalism is often replaced by programs that are "teacher proof." This is what happened to Megan and Rhonda. Another example is a reading program implemented in Sacramento, California that elicited the following response from a teacher: "I like it because the whole school is using the same lessons, the same words, the same sounds," said PZ, a second grade teacher at MH elementary. "It's consistent" (Helf, 1999). In no other profession is there a call for accountability with so little allowable professional judgment and discretion.

For some, and perhaps many teachers, these standardized approaches are an improvement on what they have been doing. Our own experience in many districts is that some teachers simply do not know very much about the teaching of reading. They need to be better equipped to teach reading.

The price to be paid is that those who excel at the higher end of the competency spectrum are being forced to forgo their own mastery. The extraordinary corollary is that many centers of excellence, exemplified by Megan and Rhonda, are literally being closed down or are struggling to survive. Megan and Rhonda, whose skills were such that they were asked to teach their peers, were also being told to do exactly what their less proficient peers were doing. The clear and obvious high level success of many individual teachers and programs is simply being ignored by states and districts as they rushed to implement standardized programs. This is destined to reduce the possible standards that the system as a whole can attain.

Many superb teachers are diminished and demoralized. The message we hear across the United States and in many other countries is the same. Those who can attain extremely high standards and who work in very complex and sophisticated ways are feeling more and more helpless and unable to do what they do well. And the frustration is felt at every level, from teachers through school administrators to the upper levels of state systems. We recently invited an exceptional teacher to coinstruct with us in a summer training program for teachers. Here is part of her faxed reply (2/16/00):

> I am having the most difficult teaching year of my career. This experience has left me feeling very inadequate as a professional. I do not feel that I am using or demonstrating brain-based instruction at this time. . . . This is not "active uncertainty." It is way too painful for that! I cannot stand up in front of a group of people and talk about what I used to do. There's no truth in that. In order to meet district pacing mandates and assessment deadlines I have taken a 15 year step backwards. After one has tasted the "fruits of [this work]" . . . there is a massive void where something spectacular used to be."

An enormous investment of time and money in developing expertise is going down the drain. The funds that were used to train teachers like Megan and Rhonda have often been wasted. The expertise developed by many superb teachers over many years, as confirmed by student results on standardized tests, is being lost to communities. And many of the best teachers, as evidenced by their student results, are looking for ways to leave teaching.

The measures being taken to ensure that mandates are complied with are creating conditions that literally make it more difficult for teachers, administrators, and students to function at their optimal psychological and professional levels. The context that is being created is making it almost impossible for new findings about learning from the neurosciences and elsewhere to actually be implemented in schools.

Many children, ranging from the ordinary to the exceptionally gifted, are being deprived of the conditions under which they thrive. The loss of gifted teachers and the standardization of programs and instruction reduces the capacity of most children to learn effectively and to reveal what they know.

What we see from the story of Megan and Rhonda, and from the larger battle in California and elsewhere, is that much of the education system is simply incapable of dealing appropriately with the complexities of information-age education. The needs have become too great for the system to satisfy, the problems have become too complex for the system to solve, and a host of questions go unanswered and issues unexamined:

- With extensive media involvement in education and with the call for school choice and technological networking expanding exponentially, teachers and educators are losing much of their traditional control of classrooms and schools. In this dynamic and turbulent environment, most command and control solutions simply cannot work.

- Although the ostensible goal of most people seeking to improve education is to "raise standards," it is not clear what "standards" mean and what high standards look like in a world where raw information doubles every two years.

- The use of tests, particularly standardized tests, to assess the quality of education begs many questions. For instance, what should be made of the fact that much of what is tested is outdated, likely never to be used and tends to be forgotten?

- The impact of the social context on educational achievement is not being dealt with adequately in public discussions. In a world where marketing and the media are so influential, what can schools really deliver?

- To what extent does society regard teachers as real professionals, particularly if minutely standardized instructional practices and procedures are mandated by districts and states as, for instance, California is doing with the teaching of reading and mathematics in the early grades?

- If some of the essential capacities being called for in the twenty-first century include creativity, individual initiative, global awareness, and more, standardization seems to be precisely the wrong approach to adopt.

- The relationship between education and the economy is not at all clear. As Alfie Kohn (2000) points out, the same U.S. education system was in place in the 1980s when Japan's economy seemed to be soaring and the United States was in a comparative slump, as in the 1990s and beyond when the United States experienced the greatest sustained economic expansion ever. Yet no one attributes the economic boom to improved education.

- Destined to severely impact all of the above, is the flood of recent research on how the brain/mind actually learns. Here, the peculiar situation that faces the United States and other nations (an issue we will explore in depth) is that one view of learning has clearly won the research battle, but an opposing and incompatible view of teaching is winning the education war.

The issues are made more urgent, and the tensions exacerbated, by the tug of very powerful interests. On one side is the call of business; on the other is the pull of home. And both drive and are driven by the world of politics.

EDUCATION'S ASTEROID: TECHNOBUSINESS

Education is becoming the business of business because it will be immensely profitable. In the past, income was earned from busing students, serving meals in the cafeteria, selling textbooks, computers, or chalk, and so on.

> The new "education industry" is about making money on actual instruction: tutoring students who have fallen behind, coaching them on the college tests and applications, delivering courses online, and taking over their classrooms or entire schools." (Walsh, 1999, p. 13)

Examples abound. Channel One, a company owned by Christopher Whittle, sends a twelve-minute newscast to more than 12,000 schools throughout the United States that can be picked up by television sets in the classroom. In addition it has a very active Web site with chat rooms, activities, and links. The price, in part, is that all the programs contain advertising that goes directly to students. Another venture, the Edison Project, seeks to have entire schools administered by a corporation under contract. Curriculum materials are created, teachers are trained, and management is undertaken by the corporation. A stated goal of the venture is for every participating school to become part of a national network, united by a common purpose and plan and linked through their technology system (Partnership School Design, 1994). In effect, the venture treats the entire United States as one electronic school district, with teachers that can readily transfer from one site to another.

The Technobusiness trend is occurring at the college and university level as well. In April 2000 a story appeared in *The Weekend Australian*, Australia's national newspaper, about a group whose expressed goal was to "exploit the explosive growth expected in 'e-education'." This made commercial sense in view of such findings as those of IBM, which forecasted a threefold (U.S.$4.5 trillion) jump in global education expenditure during the next 13 years.

The story described a global network of 18 research-intensive universities in which the News Corporation, whose chief executive is Rupert Murdoch and which publishes *The Australian*, was going to be a partner. It said that one of the network's most powerful assets was its legitimacy in China, which was created through membership of the three elite Chinese universities. News Corporation was attractive because it had a worldwide satellite network. The story also revealed that the British Government allocated £386 million in February 2000 to develop a Britain-led consortium to compete in the e-education market.

The network planned to float in 2000, and had been valued by Merrill Lynch at between U.S.$36 and $52 billion. Further partnerships with major businesses were being examined. In an interview with *The Weekend Australian* the preceding year, Professor Gilbert, University of Melbourne Vice-Chancellor, said:

> The Disneys of the world are interested, . . . It's the Microsofts, the IBMs, the News Corps, The (CNN boss) Ted Turner-type of vision of what's possible. . . . (4/22–23, 2000, p. 27)

The partnership of business and technology may have the capacity to substantially reframe public education. This seems like an impossibly grand claim, except for the enormous range of developments that are being announced and for the possibilities afforded by the World Wide Web.

> "The real excitement is in the convergence of the Internet and education," said Howard M. Block, a managing director of Banc of America Securities. "It is bordering on explosive growth." (Walsh, 1999, p. 15)

Some Examples

- Vast numbers of lesson plans in almost every subject that is regularly taught are available, many at no cost.
- Extensive quantities of raw material are also becoming available. These include interviews, archives, books, drawings, library sources, and more. Interest groups supply each other with resources and make their offerings more widely available.

- Live cameras take students into many different arenas in real time. One camera takes people into a court room in Canada, another takes people into a natural wildlife reserve in California, a third brings the space station into the classroom.
- School systems are beginning to share their strategic plans and more general materials. For example, the entire kindergarten through twelfth grade curriculum for the province of British Columbia in Canada is now on line (www.bced.gov.bc.ca/irp/)
- Parents and members of the public who have had trouble with their school systems are finding advice and support from each other, supplemented by the advice of experts, often at no cost. Topics range from help for students with special needs to support for litigation and political action.

The irony of the situation, a cruel irony perhaps, is that the public education system is opening the way for commercial development without, in general, having the faintest idea of what it is doing. One of the single largest contributing factors is the push to have every school, every classroom, every student on-line. Thus, the U.S. Department of Education seeks to provide students and teachers with access to the Internet, in part to end the isolation of teachers and, in part, to exponentially expand the resources for teaching and learning in schools and classrooms.

> It will become increasingly important to build and support network infrastructures—wired or wireless, desktop or handheld—that allow multiple devices to connect simultaneously to the Internet throughout every school building and community in the nation. (elearning, December, 2000)

The networking is being facilitated, in part, by substantial subsidies made available through a federal program called "e-learn."

Once the interactive network is in place, the opportunities are available for Technobusiness to deliver products and services that will compete ruthlessly with what public education can offer, and for education dollars. Standardization, we should add, is a boon to much of Technobusiness because it makes educational products and services so easy to develop and market, and seems to make the (very expensive) teacher expendable.

HOMESCHOOLING: THE DOMESTIC REVOLUTION

Until fairly recently, home schooling was primarily carried out by those who felt that their religion and values would not be adequately respected in public schools. There were some, however, who simply felt that public schools were not safe enough or not good enough. Both groups have swollen enormously in the past decade. In part as a result of political activism, legislation began to change so that today all 50 states in the United States permit homeschooling in some form. In 1996, according to the National Center for Education Statistics (Issues, 2000), as many as 1.4 percent of all students ages 6–17 were being homeschooled. If that rate of growth continues, it has been estimated that 10 years from now, 24 percent of American children would be homeschooled (A Coalition for Self-Learning, 2000).

Perhaps the single greatest benefit that home schooling possesses, and the single greatest threat that it poses to traditional education, is that families are free from most of the bureaucratic constraints that choke schools. The freedom is immense. And a moderately free market system is self-organizing and emerging as participants connect and support each other (A Coalition for Self-Learning, 2000).

The challenge to traditional education is more subtle than that posed by Technobusiness. The latter is bearing down on public education in some cross between an asteroid and a cloud of locusts, with the possibility of consuming, obliterating, or taking over whatever is in its path. Homeschooling families are more like an ocean rising in what was dry land. The fortifications and infrastructure of public education can simply be bypassed as homeschoolers go their own way. Both interest groups have the capacity to siphon off resources from the traditional system.

Beyond the differences between the two interests is also an enormous potential synergy. Homeschoolers have traditionally been deprived of resources, but Technobusiness is making many resources available. Parents and children now have access to extensive source material and numerous lessons prepared by teachers that are available for little or no cost. Homeschooling parents have traditionally relied on themselves for teaching and coaching, but Technobusiness can now supply additional teaching support. And homeschoolers have traditionally had limited opportunities for networking with each other and the larger community, but Technobusiness is really facilitating that networking. It is making collective homeschooling a much more viable option. Homeschooling, in fact, is flourishing as a result of the resources and links made available on the World Wide Web.

Within the rising waters there are two additional very strong currents. One is the way in which commercial programs aimed at parents can put pressure on schools. For example, in 1999, the largest selling book in the world sold some 8.5 million copies (www.thelearningweb.net). This result can be compared with a John Grisham novel that typically sells two- to three-million copies. The book was called "The Learning Revolution" (Dryden & Vos, 1993) and is a compendium of facts and strategies, mostly for pushing the envelope of the standard model, written by a New Zealand publisher and a Canadian education consultant. Almost all the copies of the book were sold to noneducators in China as the result of a campaign launched by a partnership of business and government. As the public becomes informed about this approach to teaching, parents become equipped to ask for a different approach from educators. The book is simply one leg of a multiprong assault that includes the World Wide Web, on-line coaching and courses, and more. As we write, a campaign for "The Learning Revolution" is also underway in the United States.

In addition, the homeschool movement is part of a rapidly expanding call for choice, fueled by a variety of concerns. Many parents feel that kids are unsafe in school. Many people feel that teaching in public schools is simply not good enough. In addition, there is a profound concern about values being acquired and communicated. Because homeschoolers are free of many public constraints, they are also free to combine schooling with their own spiritual pursuits. The separation of church and state does not apply. This could also provide some homeschoolers with an enormous advantage over formal education, because as we will see, one of the most powerful motivators for learning involves the pursuit of questions that matter. Public education is simply not currently equipped to deal with nor access much of the power of the search for meaning. The freedom of homeschoolers and Technobusiness to deal openly with personal, religious, and spiritual issues is a force for the expansion of both and poses an unprecedented test for the separation of church and state.

ADDITIONAL CHALLENGES FROM WITHIN

Although the thrust of most public effort is directed towards standardization of teaching and assessment, the approaches to "upgrading" the educational infrastructure are more varied. Many favor strengthening the current system by repairing and renovating buildings, supporting preschool experience, and reducing class sizes. The most extensive effort to change conditions has been the reduction in class sizes, exemplified by action in California and Tennessee. In California, for instance, no class in grades K–3 should exceed 20 students, a far cry from the high 20s or 30s. Other attempts involve safety by means varying from using weapon detectors to bolstering the presence of adults.

A strong voice is also being heard advocating far more choice about the configuration and management of schools themselves. We refer above to the spread of technology and the increasing practice of allowing private businesses to manage public schools. At least two additional trends are high on some political agendas.

Charter Schools

Charter schools are moderately independent components of the public school system, run by the groups who create them under the supervision of some state-authorized chartering agency. In 1991 there was one charter school in the United States. As we approach the middle of 2001 there are more than 2,000, and there is a widespread call for more. While, the degree of freedom and flexibility offered by the different states under the guise of charter schools varies enormously (Finn, Manno, & Vanourek, 2000), enthusiasm for charter schools in the United States is very strong.

Vouchers

A voucher is like a food stamp. It is a coupon that can be spent by parents at the school of choice. There are many different types of voucher programs. At the time of writing, vouchers are in effect to a limited extent in Florida. They were on the ballot in 2000 but were rejected in Michigan and California. Vouchers bridge what has been a very wide gap between public education on the one hand and homeschooling and religious education on the other, because under some programs, parents of children in public schools that are "failing" would receive vouchers to use at their own discretion—say for tuition fees at a private school or to employ extra help for their children.

Part of the confusion permeating public education is caused by the fact that neither charter schools nor vouchers mean the same thing to everyone, including those who promote them. For example, one voucher initiative would have simply provided parents of every child with a voucher, irrespective of how well the child's school was doing, while another initiative would provide vouchers to parents of children in failing schools. Adding fuel to the mix are very strong ideological differences, often expressed in passionate and, sometimes, corrosive language, most being picked up and amplified by the media and used in political campaigns. The left accuses the right of profiteering, privatization, and destruction of the common educational foundation on which democracy depends; the right accuses the left of acting like big brother and imposing values that only parents should select.

HOW PEOPLE LEARN—THE PROMISE OF BRAIN RESEARCH

It is just conceivable that the turbulence and confusion may also be the good news. It is possible that after the storm has passed there will be the sort of genuinely high-caliber education for the public that is desperately needed. It was, after all, the extinction of the dinosaurs that paved the way for the rise of mammals and the appearance of humans. As they enter into the information age, most societies are changing dramatically with education at their core, and because the standard model simply does not work to achieve anything approaching what might be called high standards, something new has a very good chance of emerging.

The way to begin is to rethink the basic assumptions that are used to guide decisions and frame solutions. The place to begin, so much overlooked in the bulk of public discussion, is with how people learn.

The central point is that there are several natural ways in which people learn. Most of them are ignored by traditional education. Some of them are exploited by business. Some of them are known and used — explicitly or intuitively — by the really great teachers. Some of them are used quite naturally by really good homeschooling families. Those ways are now becoming more visible.

The 1990s witnessed an immense proliferation of published reports about how the human brain works. That research is helping to organize and make sense of a century of research in psychology that has examined different aspects of the mind. For example (as will be shown in more detail in chapters 3 and 4):

- Brains do not function like machines. Brains are living systems which means that their primary goal is to survive and adapt — even in a classroom.
- People do not learn only what they concentrate on. Everyone picks up information unintentionally, and processes much of it unconsciously.

- Emotions and thought are deeply intertwined, and every concept and idea is always shaped by how people feel. A sterile emotional climate is not neutral—it literally shapes understanding, often twisting it or preventing it.
- Some of the most primitive drives that all people have, such as fight or flight in times of emergency, interfere with optimal learning. Yet in the highly stressed world that most of us inhabit, fight or flight is rampant, and ineffective learning is an inevitable consequence.
- Every brain emerges out of a unique set of genes and is shaped by unique experiences. While common programs are legitimate, standardized instruction for all is fundamentally absurd, and yet that is the direction that most school reform is taking.

In essence, much of what has been taken for granted about learning and teaching is being called into question, and yet most of the educational reforms that flood the family of nations fail to even consider the new findings, let alone benefit from them.

THE FOUNDATION FOR HIGH
STANDARDS IS REAL-WORLD PERFORMANCE

We will show in chapter 3 that the biological basis of learning is to make it possible for people to survive and thrive in the real world. This capacity is generally a function of *dynamic* or *performance knowledge* or what neuroscientist Elkonen Goldberg calls *adaptive knowledge.* There is an enormous difference between *surface* or *static knowledge* (somewhat like the philosopher Alfred North Whitehead called inert fact), which tends not to change, and performance knowledge, which is the basis of how people interact in the world and engage in life. The primary purpose of education should be to increase the capacity of individuals and groups to survive and thrive by developing performance knowledge. The main defect of the standard model is that it tends to generate surface knowledge.

The challenge is deceptively simple and takes us back to a dispute that has been ongoing for a century. The way to develop performance knowledge—the real knowledge that people actually use in everyday life—always involves a combination of direct instruction and lived experience. Anyone who ever masters any idea or skill to a level of genuine competence always receives some direct instruction (though sometimes just from books) and also has opportunities for real experience. We should add that abstract and complex ideas and sophisticated intellectual skills can also be static or dynamic. They, too, become dynamic when they become part of lived experience in ways that we illustrate in chapters 5 and 6.

The primary question, then, is how to integrate direct instruction and authentic experience in education, and how to manage the task in such a turbulent and changing world? For most of the twentieth century, schooling and everyday experience existed in two distinct domains. Schooling came first and life experience followed or was peripheral. The challenge, now, is to integrate the two.

The difference is analogous to the difference between the impact of traditional Newtonian physics and quantum mechanics. The former establishes the principles that explain how machines work; the latter is based on what happens when the atom is split. When the atom is split much more power is made available than comes from any machine working according to Newton's laws. However, in the early years quantum mechanics was not understood and the theory was even suspect. Next, experiments began to validate the theory. Then, about forty years after the theory first emerged it became possible to split the atom. And today we have the power of the atom at our fingertips. The trouble is that public education does not have another century available to get things right.

In education, the difference between traditional direct instruction and instruction embedded in lived experience is equivalent to a quantum leap in what can be accomplished by teachers, parents, and administrators with students. Unfortunately, just as in physics in the early days, many parents, educators, and policymakers simply don't understand the complexities involved, and don't know how to implement experience-based education well, especially on a large scale. That is partly why attempts seem to fail so often. The problem is compounded because people who don't know what they are doing talk as though they do. This reveals itself clearly in the debates about the teaching of reading and the use and abuse of a practice called whole language, a topic that we will revisit from time to time.

THE FUTURE OF EDUCATION

Where paradoxes flourish and uncertainty abounds, the odds are that the limits of a way of thinking have been reached. Almost all of those seeking to improve education, even those advocating more choice, are still in the grip of a set of inadequate beliefs.

We will take the competing visions of how people learn as our starting point. This book argues that in most classrooms, in much of Technobusiness, and in many homes, a primitive version of the standard model is prevailing, and that, as a consequence of the standardization movement, public education is rapidly moving in a direction that will probably see test scores rise at the lower end of the competency spectrum, but which has no conceivable way of substantially raising competence and understanding generally. In fact there is a very strong possibility that, notwithstanding the best efforts of many people, in some respects, real standards will decline significantly across the board. However the decline will be obscured because standardized tests are so narrowly focused. This result is unacceptable for parents who care about their children, for businesses that need skilled workers and creative managers, for states and nations whose democratic systems depend on a well-educated population.

The Guided Experience Approach

While the standard model can be improved substantially, it has inherent limitations that make it impossible to achieve the quality of education for which so many thirst. Fortunately, there is an alternative. The *guided experience approach* marries the twin processes of direct instruction and experience-based learning. Chapters 3 through 6 are devoted to explaining and describing the guided experience approach.

The foundation, as we will see, is improved community in classrooms, homes, schools, in neighborhoods. The reason is that emotion and relationship are at the heart of effective intellectual functioning. One practical consequence is that schools need to be relatively small and social coherence within the school community relatively strong. Equally as important is safety and the satisfaction of basic needs. Unfortunately, as we will see, many of the most frequently touted strategies for improving the standard model actually decrease a sense of safety in both students and adults and so are counter productive. There is no doubt that the price to be paid for slightly increasing test scores will be a decrease in other important ways of functioning, including creative thinking and the willingness and ability to take risks.

Within a well-established learning community a host of processes for improving teaching and administration can be developed. We will describe some of these practices and procedures in more depth in succeeding chapters. The key is to provide students with complex activities and ongoing experiences in which the curriculum is embedded. Teachers who have high standards and who know what needs to be mastered by students, use questions and other processes to guide students in research, investigations, and practice. The guided-experience approach is flexible and therefore seems messy, but it is extremely powerful when done well. However, conditions must be created that make it possible for the approach to be successful, not least of which is an intelligent approach to testing and assessment. Assessment of students by observing them in real-world performance is the key to ascertaining what they really know. To the extent that society demands standardized tests, they must always be secondary and not the focus of attention.

The Added Power of Alignment

There is a way of further improving education by an order of magnitude. There are ways for the power and potential of Technobusiness and homeschooling to be integrated with public systems of education that genuinely open themselves for change. There are ways for parents, businesses, and communities to come together and provide education for large numbers of people at a much higher level then now occurs. There is a way to incorporate the best of what is known about learning and teaching in the emergent future.

The key will turn out to be alignment between the best beliefs and practices of the broader culture and the best beliefs and practices of education. We introduce the notion of alignment in chapter 4 and expand on it in depth in subsequent chapters. Brain research confirms that the context teaches. While the standard model may preach initiative and high standards, children in the standard model are constantly immersed in a context that squelches initiative and rewards conformity and lower standards. The challenge is to support an approach to education in which the best of the larger culture is lived and expressed in schooling itself. That is when schools are what they need to be—apprentice communities. When the dynamic aspects of a culture are aligned with the guided experience approach to learning and teaching, many brakes on learning are released and an enormous degree of previously invisible capacity in students, educators, and communities is accessed. And that is what has to be accomplished in order to successfully navigate through, and prosper in, the twenty-first century.

CHAPTER 2

The Standard Model—Back to the Future?

At 9:30 on a Wednesday morning, 19 kindergartners sit on the floor around teacher Josie Costa [in Dwight Elementary School in Hartford, Connecticut] as she goes over a story about a dog named "Sad Sam." The teacher reads the narrative, prompting the students—who have their own copies of the book—to chime in with the dialogue. When Ms. Costa reads that the dog's owner loves Sam, but doesn't love that he jumps in puddles, they call out: "No, Sam! No."

An almost identical scene is unfolding in nearly every one of Hartford's elementary schools at about the same time. Kindergartners through the city are reading today about Sad Sam and his propensity for puddle jumping. . . .

The "codified" approach shows up not just in elementary school. Middle school math teachers, for example, have "progress schedules" to help them keep their lessons on track with the rest of the system.

Pedagogically, many educators here say, the standardized approach makes sense for a district in which families—many of whom are recent immigrants—move around so frequently. . . .

"Why would you have one school handling things differently from another?" [a principal] said. "If a child leaves and goes elsewhere in the city, they can just call up their old teacher here and say, 'What level is he at?'" (Archer, 2000, p. 18–19)

In the thirty thousand years prior to the Renaissance and the Industrial Revolution—for hunter gatherers, farmers, crafts people, and others—the way of learning and teaching was simple. Loosely speaking, all groups used some type of apprenticeship. Management guru Peter Senge once wrote that people who did not know hung around with people who did know. Children hung around with adults, and played at being adults. And they learned, picking up knowledge and skills by observation, by modeling, and just from being with people who were doing the things they would learn.

Of course, many adults also provided direct instruction and coaching to children and apprentices. The apprenticeship model is marvelously adaptable, with direct instruction tailored to suit the development of the student. The instruction was scaffolded, and always went hand in glove with practice—practice—practice. And the measure of success was the extent to which the product or performance matched the work of the master.

A third element was also interwoven into this fabric of learning. Beyond the play in context and the direct instruction in a skill or craft was initiation into a larger way of life. Often this took the form of ceremonies and rituals conducted by Elders. And some of it involved stories where youngsters were invited to enter into experience, inducing a sort of respect that teachers and parents of today yearn for:

> Learning from nature and from an Elder involves a special quality of silence and alert watchfulness. The respect one shows to an Elder acts to create that area of quietness and receptivity into which the Elder can speak. (Peat, 1996, p. 74)

In this way the stories of the past, the culture, the values, and the more general practices of life were introduced, preserved, and carried forward.

The systems were not necessarily kind or gentle, and they varied in how effective they were. But that was how they worked. Instruction and experience intermingled in a multiplicity of ways, with learning occurring in "real time" as a child grew into adulthood.

There were also schools. In many parts of the ancient world, libraries and great centers for formal learning developed. And for many centuries schools of a sort existed in Europe. They were places where people gathered in relatively organized ways to receive instruction in matters of the arts and the mind. Often the recipients of instruction were those who wanted to learn (or the children of parents who wanted their children taught) and private teachers were hired for that purpose.

THE RISE OF PUBLIC EDUCATION

Times change in complex ways. This is not a history of the development of schools. (For differing views of such a history, readers might like to see Coulson, 1999 or Abbott and Ryan, 2000). However, a set of needs and practices arose over a period of centuries that led almost inexorably to the schools and education systems that we have today. We referred to it previously as the standard model.

Reading and Writing Made Information Available to All

Reading was not always a fact of life, and writing even less so. Although artists used symbols as early as thirty thousand years ago, reading and writing developed within the last six thousand years. And it was with the development of the printing press (in the fifteenth century in Europe and much earlier in China) that reading became fairly widespread because of "speed, uniformity of texts and relative cheapness" (Manguel, 1996, p.134). The primary use in the early years was religious as it became possible for many people to gain access to religious texts. Even within the last century the nature of and reasons for reading have changed, and it has only been in relatively recent times that reading has become a prerequisite for success in almost every sphere of endeavor.

Part of the power of the written word is that the stories told by elders, and the information acquired by experts become available at a distance, though still second hand. Everyone can access the material. And much of it needs to be accessed by people who do not have an elder or expert to call on directly. In essence, it became necessary and possible to transmit information on a very large scale. And it became essential to be able to receive, interpret, and make use of that information. The ability to read therefore emerged as a foundational attribute, even more necessary today than it has ever been.

Masses Needed Training

In the industrial era, accompanied as it was by a host of other factors, such as the move of people to cities, apprenticeships in families, villages, and tribes became impossible. Sets of skills had to be mastered that were new, or that could not be taught in traditional ways. Ways and places had to be developed where many people could simultaneously acquire the sets of skills that were needed by industrial society. Some of the training occurred in the work place, but literacy and numeracy in particular required teachers and places for them to teach.

Society Mandated Schooling

Earlier societies had no doubt that everyone needed to grasp the stories, the rules, the rituals, and the practices that made it possible to live together. Socialization was taken for granted, and initiation of various kinds was vital to the young and to their elders.

In more recent times, schooling has become one of the means of transmitting culture and socializing children.

> For most countries in Europe and North America learning became irreversibly equated with formal systematic schooling sometime during the middle to late 19th century. This blurring of schooling and learning was a direct result of national governments using "formal systems of education" to develop loyal, productive and socially contented citizens. (Abbott & Ryan, 2000, p.78)

Even more recently, surging after the end of the Second World War, schools became the means by which states prepared children for work and advanced study. The core curriculum was established as a prerequisite for all children, and 'reading, 'riting, and 'rithmatic came to be regarded as indispensable for success.

Preparation before Participation

The thrust was not participation *in* work and life but preparation *for* work and life. In the preindustrial world, children and novices lived through the ventures of adults. If not in on the hunt, they were in on the return of the hunters and in the preparation and consumption of what was gathered. The dances and celebrations and play and stories related directly to experience. As information became more abstract, as skills were applied at a distance from the home, as the sheer volume of information and the complexity of trades and professions increased, it became necessary to prepare children for what they would encounter in the future but in the absence of direct experience. Stories were written down, and the teacher became the story teller—but the stories were out of context. The facts became facts "about" and not personally lived. And the skills were taught in isolation, not in the course of work or art. Thus school separated itself from life.

Most Countries, First—Second—and Third World, Adopted the Standard Model of Education

Schools have become the places where large numbers of children and students are presented with roughly similar facts and skills in roughly similar ways. In general, that instruction in school has very little connection with whatever else is going on in a child's life. Schooling has been divorced from experience, with the usually unstated assumption that the actual life experience that students need will be plentiful after school is over. Some people tried to combine the two. Thomas Dewey was one, and there are schools such as the Samuel Sewall Greeley School in Winetka, Illinois that implement his philosophy very successfully. Another was Maria Montessori whose dictum was "follow the child." In general, however, the notion of bringing everyday experience into schooling has been largely discounted, generally (it is said) because it does not "work."

TRADITIONAL TEACHING: THE WAY IT'S ALWAYS BEEN DONE

> The traditional method (often called "direct instruction") is that a knowledgeable teacher—usually with the aid of a textbook—introduces a new idea or concept, shows how it works, and then assigns problems that students solve using this new information. Through much practice, students deepen their understanding and accumulate fundamental skills. Teachers expect children to commit basic facts and formulas to memory. In traditional classrooms, partial credit is often given for using reasonable methods to solve test problems, but grades rest largely on finding the right answers. (Bennett, Finn, & Cribb, 1999, p. 320)

The model of instruction described by Bennet is very much what teachers were left with once lived experience was divorced from instruction. Several elements need to be identified:

1. *Curriculum (standards).* The central organizing idea is the subject or field of study. A core curriculum is developed that embraces the essential concepts, facts, and skills deemed necessary for a basic education. In the United States the core curriculum tends to include the language arts, math, science, and social studies.

The focus of the current standardization movement is essentially a meeting of experts and others to reorganize and repackage the curriculum.

2. Instruction. The teacher's job is to take the knowledge and skills developed by experts, and which they, the teachers, have mastered, and then to show and tell the students how to master it as well. That is why it is called direct instruction. Because the material is quite complex, it is broken down into manageable units that are prepared as lessons, and in this way a full course can be covered.

Clear learning objectives are spelled out for the course as a whole, and for each specific lesson. Lessons need to be organized in what Bennett et al. call a "carefully planned sequence" (p. 595). But because design and delivery can be difficult, there are many techniques that mentors share with novices in how to go about teaching effectively.

3. Consolidation. Teachers teach and students learn. In essence, the specific responsibility of students is to consolidate and internalize what they are given by teachers. They do so by listening, taking notes, doing tasks and problems set by the teacher and by practice—practice—practice.

Much of the actual practice is done through homework. Students therefore need a set of basic study skills to help them learn and remember, and a set of life management skills so that they can organize their time to do what needs to be done. One of the traditional roles of parents has been to ensure that homework gets done.

4. Maintain discipline. Using the standard model, it is really difficult to teach one student, let alone 30 at one time. Much teacher education therefore focuses on the skills of classroom management. These range from improved delivery techniques (to gain and hold student attention) to methods for ensuring compliance and good behavior. One reason why students have been seated in rows facing the front of the classroom is so that teachers can see what students are doing and make sure that they are attending. Traditionally, a good, effective classroom is reflected in quiet and attentive students who do what they are told, when they are told.

5. Assessment. Educators, parents, and the community want to know what students have actually learned, so learning is assessed. The basic method of assessment is a test in each subject, usually taken at the end of a course or year. Traditionally a report card is issued with a number or letter that shows roughly how well a student did. Proud parents often carry bumper stickers, for example, saying that "my child is an honor student at xyz school."

SCHOOLS AS SOCIAL MACHINES

Teaching one child is difficult, teaching 30 is a real challenge. How, then, does one teach—say—one hundred thousand? It is not a surprise that we talk about the education system. The only way that most people knew how to deliver education to all children was to do it systematically. That meant using the system technology that prevailed in the nineteenth and early twentieth century. And the technology that towered over all at the time was the technology of the machine—the conveyor belt—the processes that worked like clockwork.

In fact there have been several related ways of organizing people so that they work together, all of which were popular in the nineteenth century, and some of which have much more ancient roots. They all came together beautifully in public education.

Armies: For millennia people have sought ways to organize armies and fight wars. The Roman army, for instance, was extremely well organized. It had a supreme leader with a hierarchy of leadership. Troops were organized into manageable groups. Total obedience was expected and maintained by hard discipline. And success depended on people mastering their functions and working together. The system was so organized that people could be trained very well for their functions, and could be replaced quite readily if they fell in battle. In the nineteenth century, the Prussian army was similarly organized. And in early twentieth-century America, Horace Mann looked long and hard at the Prussian military model as a method of organizing schools.

Factories: The nineteenth century provided, and the twentieth century perfected, factories. These were places where clear goals were set, products were planned and produced, workers and managers had well-laid-out jobs, work could be programmed and timed and sequenced, products could be identified and assessed or graded, and a whole set of devices could be developed for motivating people to work hard and punishing them for failure. Thus early curriculum thinkers such as Bobbit and Charters in the 1920s, explicitly based their work on ideas of "industrial scientist" F. W. Taylor.

Sociology: A German sociologist, Max Weber, helped to consolidate the picture. One element he added was the notion of the flow of information. He suggested that the best way to get work done was to have it allocated to people whose jobs were clearly defined. They would be organized in a hierarchy, with small and detailed jobs carried out by many people at the bottom, and larger and more general jobs carried out by fewer people at the top. Information would flow up and down the hierarchy, and people would only be told what they needed to know in the particular job and at the particular level where they worked.

Weber called the process that he developed a bureaucracy. We can call it a social machine. The model is powerful, extremely elegant, and in many ways it has been very successful. In theory it became possible to funnel every child in every family through the same type of system. And it is beautifully illustrated by the changes that have been very recently made in the Hartford school district in Connecticut with which the chapter begins.

A central organizing authority is set up, empowered by the state to administer satellite centers that are called schools. There is always a hierarchy, with policy set at the top and specific tasks carried out by those below. Some type of regional division is necessary. The hierarchy is usually something like this: State, district, school, head teachers, teachers, teacher aids, student, parent.

Students are initially organized into clusters and cohorts that could be organized and managed. This is done by using the calendar year as a basic organizer, and then dividing children according to age and grade. So most children who complete high school begin school when they are about 6, continue through 12 years, and leave when they are about 18.

Within each school there is an enormously complex task of planning classes for all students. Consequently much administration focuses on managing small parcels of time to accommodate the many needs. Classes usually take the form of 45- to 55-minute blocks for each subject several times each week.

Qualified teachers need to be hired, all of whom are certified to be competent to teach prescribed material. The basic way of ensuring compliance with this requirement is to set up a system of credentials, administered by the state in some association with organizations that train teachers.

While they have a moderate degree of professional discretion, there is also a central way of teaching that is shared by most. It is the model of direct instruction described above.

All of this activity occurrs in physical plant appropriate for the purpose. They are the schools that we have today—buildings, most of which look like factories—usually accompanied by some facility for sport and larger gatherings.

IS THE SYSTEM BROKEN—AND DOES IT NEED FIXING?

The prevailing concern in the mind of the public is that the standard model (though it is not called that) is not working well enough. It may be broken, and it needs fixing. Issues range from the well-being of kids to their academic success.

Safety: On April 20, 1999, a horrific episode of school violence in Columbine High School, in Littleton, Colorado, traumatized the nation nearly as much as the local inhabitants. Two adolescents opened fire on their classmates, killing 13 and wounding 21. This was one of several occasions of lethal violence at schools over the years that has many parents and the larger community worried about violence at school and the safety of children.

Values: A second concern has to do with discipline and values. Some parents and educators feel that a large number of students are unruly beyond tolerable bounds, that they are discourteous to the public and that the values that they are picking up or are being taught are inconsistent with what a "good" child should be. Other parents feel that their children are too passive and unthinking. The intriguing point is that parents with radically different political views express a common concern about the values and attitudes being taught in schools.

Literacy: It has long been known that a significant proportion of American adults are illiterate to some extent. Numbers are difficult to spell out because there is a continuum of illiteracy: some cannot even recognize single letters such as "a" or "z"; others can read stories but do not grasp nuances nor read critically for hidden beliefs that are being promoted. The red flag in all this is that many of those who are functionally illiterate in some way have had up to 12 years of school!

Just How Good Are Our Schools Anyway?

Whether or not schools work, or work well enough, has been the subject of bitter debate for many years in many countries. Respected educators differ strongly with each other. The various interest groups mentioned in chapter 1 weigh into the dispute vigorously. The question is aired repeatedly in the press, on television, over the Web, and in private discussions.

The question is legitimate and important. Parents want to know. Government wants to know. Industry wants to know. Interest groups want to know. People asking that question want a reliable, honest, objective answer. They want to know how well their kids or their school or their state compares with others. They also want educators and the system to be accountable for results. And beneath it all is the gnawing fear that the system really is not performing well enough.

Again Hartford illustrates the way that it works. The district had been in turmoil, and its test scores were the lowest in the state. When the new superintendent was hired in 1998, he pledged that the district would never be so shamed again. The changes that he implemented were specifically intended to prove themselves in terms of improved test scores. His story is repeated throughout the United States and much of the rest of the world.

Perhaps the most important factor causing disquiet is the comparison of U.S. students with their counterparts overseas. The most widely cited comparative analysis is TIMSS, the Third International Mathematics and Science Study released in 1995.

> U.S. students scored above the international average in both mathematics and science at the fourth-grade level. At the eighth-grade level, U.S. students performed above the international average in science and below the international average in mathematics. In the final year of secondary school (twelfth grade in the U.S.), U.S. performance was among the lowest in both science and mathematics, including among our most advanced students. (www.nces.ed.gov/timss/timss95/index.asp)

These results have become a rallying point for those seeking world class standards for all U.S. students. Thus, 15 years after the publication of *A Nation at Risk*, The National Center for Education Reform declared (1998), on the basis of the TIMSS results, that although economic issues had changed,

> This evidence suggests that, compared to the rest of the industrialized world, our students lag seriously in critical subjects vital to our future. That's a national shame.

The TIMSS-Repeat was released in December 2000 (nces.ed. gov/pubsearch). It dealt exclusively with eighth graders, and showed that American schoolchildren fail to sustain their fourth-grade standing. Seventeen countries had fourth graders take TIMSS in 1995, and then had eighth graders retake in 1999. Within that cohort of 17 countries, the now eighth graders from the United States were in the bottom tier in math, and below average in science.

The picture is more complicated than it first appears, however. After looking at TIMSS-R results, noted researcher David Berliner points out that

In science, 26 nations outperformed Mississippi, and 37 nations beat the District [of Columbia] . . . But only one nation, Singapore, scored above Colorado, Connecticut, Iowa, Maine [and 11 other states]. (Berliner, 2001)

In short, the picture is mixed. Nevertheless, in answer to the question, "Just how good are U.S. schools anyway," the consensus answer appears to be, "not nearly good enough." And that concern spills over into states, districts, and local communities.

TAKING ACTION TO RAISE SCORES

The goal that drives education reform at this point in time is to raise all student scores on standardized tests—particularly reading, writing, and math. The standard model itself is not in question. The general perception is the model is not working well enough, and needs fixing. Among the actual changes that have occurred recently or are being seriously contemplated are the following:

Content standards (curriculum): At least 49 states have significantly added to what they ask of students, though there are varying degrees of complexity and difficulty in the standards set. In addition, many subject area associations such as the NCTM (National Council of Teachers of Mathematics) have reformulated standards for schools.

High-stakes standardized tests: In parallel with the development of standards has been the deployment of more standardized tests, many occurring annually at most grade levels. In California it is called the Stanford Nine. The Texas counterpart is the TAAS. Almost all states have them, and almost all have a very high component of multiple choice, fact-based questions.

Accountability: As standards are set for students and schools, and as accountability becomes more important, provision is being made at state and federal levels for identifying bad schools—and for "fixing" them. In some cases administrators are removed. In some cases, additional training and consultation is required. In some cases schools are taken over in their entirety by district or state.

Teacher training: Almost every candidate in the turn-of-the-millennium political campaigns advocated more teacher training, and the trend continues. Although numerous changes and processes have been introduced; however, they are almost always reduced to practices that reflect the standard model. For example, in California a great deal of money is funneled into training teachers to teach literacy, but those using a less standardized, intense, and complex language experience called "whole language" are excluded by law from being funded by the state. One problem is that whole language is a bit like cholesterol—there is good and bad whole language. It takes years to master good whole language (appropriate when one looks at the time taken to master any profession). However, the preferred training for the teaching of reading now focuses on specific, prescriptive programs and packages such as "Success for All" or "Open Court." In these programs the precise daily actions and activities for teachers are spelled out and can be monitored and controlled in much the same way as assembly-line workers can be supervised.

The larger system: While the standardization movement is heavily prescriptive as to content, teaching, and assessment, many of the solutions for choosing and managing schools proposed by those in the standardization movement provide for substantial freedom of choice. One tendency is to focus on improving resources and the infrastructure of public education, another is to provide more options. Charter schools (for profit and not-for profit), vouchers, and business management of public schools are all being tried. Partnering all of these will be the increase of distance education in many forms. Though not new (children in remote places in Australia and Alaska went to school by radio decades ago), the proliferation and sophistication of high-tech distance education can bring unprecedented resources to the ordinary school and student.

ARE SCORES RISING?

As mentioned, the instrument of choice of the standardization movement is the standardized test. For example, a story in *Newsweek* on "The Truth About Testing" (Lehman, 1999, p. 65) has this to say: "Standardized tests are a necessary tool in the fixing of American Education."

Such tests are believed to be scientific and many of the tools of science are invoked. The variables (say student knowledge of a particular subject) are identified. Tests are developed that either compare student knowledge to some criterion identified by experts in the field or to how well other students do. The conditions for evaluating student knowledge (perhaps a two-hour test to be taken at the end of eighth grade) are prescribed. The tests are administered and scored, and results are then publicized and compared.

For the time being we will not examine the underlying beliefs for using standardized tests (a topic we visit in chapter 7) though in our opinion, most of the time such testing is an inappropriate and a misleading way of assessing students, schools, and programs. The core issue is that standardized tests are endorsed by politicians, the media, and most members of the public, and the results of students and schools on standardized tests are the lynchpin of the standardization movement.

At the time of writing, there is considerable self-congratulation in the press in several states about the raising of test scores. Most highly touted are the improvements in Texas. The overview of student performances issued by the Texas Education Agency (1999–2000), on the 1999 TAAS reported "an upward trend in achievement at all grade levels."

Although attempts to compare results from different states are very difficult they are also undertaken in a variety of ways. The major sources of information in the United States are the National Assessment of Educational Progress (NAEP) tests. One study conducted by the RAND Corporation, based on the NAEP tests given between 1990 and 1996 and published in July 2000 suggested that

> The education reforms of the 1980s and 1990s seem to be working . . . but some states are doing far better than others in making achievement gains and in elevating their students' performance compared with students of similar racial and socioeconomic background in other states. Texas and Indiana are high performers on both these counts. (Grissmer, Flanagan, Kawata, & Williamson, 2000)

Their study focused primarily on math with insufficient information being available on reading.

> Math scores are rising across the country at a national average rate of about one percentile point per year, a pace outstripping that of the previous two decades. . . . Progress is far from uniform, however. One group of states—led by North Carolina and Texas and including Michigan, Indiana and Maryland—boasts gains about twice as great as the national average. Another group—including Wyoming, Georgia, Delaware and Utah—shows minuscule gains or none at all. Most states fall in between.

The authors of the study subsequently looked at 1998 scores on math and reading, and their preliminary observation was that the trend was continuing.

SOMETHING ABOUT THE SCORES DOES NOT ADD UP

While some test scores may be increasing according to some indicators, all is not well. By way of contrast to the RAND and Texas studies mentioned above, two other studies cast some doubt on their findings. First, one 30-year study issued by the U.S. Department of Education based on NAEP results showed that reading scores were essentially unchanged, and math scores only rose marginally (NAEP 1999 Trends in Academic Progress, 1999). Second, another RAND study released in October, 2000 examined results in Texas in particular, and it called into question some of the findings in the first study referred to above. The researchers compared the way that students educated in Texas and students educated in other states did on non-Texas tests, and they found that the Texas students performed no better than the non-Texas students. The researchers talk about "the stark differences between the stories told by NAEP and TAAS" (Klein, Hamilton, McCoffrey, & Strecher, 2000).

Indeed, there are indications of a much greater problem that standardization is exacerbating (Meier, 2000; Kohn, 2000). Because Texas has been promoted as a model state, we use other sources of statistics on Texas in order to show that results may be clouded.

Drop out rates are very high. The exit exam in Texas takes place in 10th grade, and Texas' own reports indicate that pass rates are climbing significantly for that test. However, according to Haney, one reason for the rise in scores is that an increasing number of students, a disproportionate number being minorities, are being retained at the end of 9th grade, and then drop out before taking the 10th grade exam (Haney, 2000). Drop out rates are important because the more that weak students drop out, the higher the overall scores seem to go, even if there is no actual improvement!

Many students are unprepared by school for college. For example:

> More than one-third of Texas freshmen who attend state colleges or universities are so ill-prepared that they must take remedial courses. (Norris, 1999)

While the problem of ill-prepared college-bound students has been with us for many years, results on the SAT (scholastic aptitude test) for Texas have also remained static. If rising scores on school tests have not led to any increase in the quality of students entering college, one implication is that there has not been a genuine increase in proficiency.

Total reliance on standardized tests may lead to a reduction in the quantity and quality of material being taught. McNeil and Valenzuela (2000) report that subjects tested by TAAS (reading, writing, and mathematics) are being reduced to isolated fragments of fact and skills. So, some high school teachers report that practice for TAAS has raised the pass rate for the reading section of TAAS at their schools, but "many of their students are unable to use those same skills for actual reading" (p. 6). A suggestion from the RAND report that calls into question improvements in Texas is that Texas students had simply been trained to answer questions covered specifically by Texas tests, which is why the students seemed to have improved. In addition, there is increasing evidence that subjects not tested on standardized tests are receiving less attention then they used to receive (See, for instance, *ABC News,* Norris, 1999; Portner, 2000).

Prescriptive, standardized teaching programs may significantly reduce student skills. Research has been conducted (Moustafa & Hand, 2000) on a very prescriptive reading program called *Open Court* that is used prolifically. It shows that "In every measure used in this study, schools using *Open Court* did not do as well on the SAT 9 reading assessments as schools using the nonscripted programs in this study" (p. 9).

Disparities between the results of white and students of color in Texas may not be decreasing as TAAS results suggest, but may be increasing, as the RAND report on results in Texas indicate. For example, nearly 16 percent of African American students and nearly 17 percent of latinos leave school after 9th grade rather than enter 10th grade, as compared to just over 8 percent of white students (Haney, 2000).

There are other signs, often anecdotal, that something is badly wrong with the results produced by the standard model. Readers can test this for themselves simply by talking with friends and colleagues. For example:

- Much of what seems to be learned according to tests simply does not transfer into useful skill and knowledge in the real world. That may be why some people who perform magnificently on tests fail at life.
- Much of what people learned on tests is totally forgotten, often within weeks. We have explored this issue informally by asking thousands of people at our keynotes, lectures, and seminars this question: Why did you study at school? "For the test," they answer in unison. We then ask, what happened after the test? "We forget," they reply.
- Many people who flunk tests and even drop out of school do superbly in the real world, even on subjects that they failed at school. There are many anecdotal examples, such as successful stockbrokers and even bookmakers who performed poorly in school math but flourish in the world of real math.

As we stand back for a better view of what is happening in education, some of the troubling features of the standard model as it is currently operating become visible. Let us look from two different vantage points.

First, at least 15 percent of federal expenditures on education serve special needs. This is not a criticism of those seeking additional assistance. It simply leads to the question of how many special needs are indicative of individual problems or of a system that is failing. For example, in 1994 about 6 percent of boys and 1.5 percent of girls were diagnosed with Attention Deficit/Hyperactivity Disorder (Swanson, et al., 1998). Of course, some of those diagnoses are correct. However, vast number of the children said to lack the ability to pay attention for any length of time can spend hours totally focused on projects and games that interest them. Moreover, young children are naturally active. For both reasons, it looks very much as though the frequent diagnosis of ADHD is telling us that the larger system can not cope with normal child behavior such as vigorous activity or play essential for brain and body development. Similarly, many other cases of apparent learning disabilities in individuals may be evidence of the dysfunction of the system. The extreme case may be that sometimes the administration of Ritalin is the use of a drug by the system to make sure that kids behave.

Second, the world inhabited by kids has changed dramatically. Television was invented in 1926 and became popular several years after the Second World War. Nowadays, the average child in the United States watches more than 19 hours of television a week—almost 1,000 hours a year (Kids & Media, 1999). This means that he or she spends nearly the same number of hours in front of television as in the classroom each year. It is also estimated that the average child also watches between 20,000 and 40,000 commercials a year (Leonhardt & Kerwin, 1997). This is time when they are not playing outdoors (unless involved in a formally organized sports program) or otherwise physically and emotionally active rather than passive. We also now know that major film studios have systematically targeted underage children as audiences for R-rated films (Fiore, 2000).

When we add to the above the time spent by children on video games and computers, we begin to see them growing up in a profoundly different world—a world awash in attention-getting, fast-paced entertainment. Yet heavy television viewing has been correlated with stifled creativity, a shorter attention span, and with interfering with skills necessary for reading, listening, and writing (Duncan, 1998). The point is that the everyday experience of children is clearly having an impact on how they learn and function, and yet the standard model addresses very few of those additional factors.

IMPLICATIONS

Even if its basic assumptions are accepted, it is clear that the standard model is uneven. Some do it well, some do it poorly. It is equally clear that when attempts are made to improve the standard model, no state can rely on its own practices and its own tests to tell the full story of what is happening in its system of education. Although standardized tests are inadequate guides, for reasons we will spell out later, it is clear that there should be some kind of cross-referencing before large claims can be made about how well any entity is doing. A good way to do this is to have students from one school or state engage in some comparative activity with students from another school or state.

In addition, something much more dramatic is becoming visible. The issues just addressed collectively suggest that even the best of the standard model is inadequate. Thus, even in Japan, whose eighth graders regularly rank near the top in international comparisons in math and science, there is evidence that many students hate both subjects, and there is some concern that teaching is too conformist and their programs are not producing those qualities and abilities essential for practical success in a rapidly changing world (Magnier, 2001). One implication for the United States is that the standardization movement is actually making the situation in education worse.

The point is confirmed by the fact that many teachers, programs, and schools produce absolutely outstanding results, despite not following the prescriptive path demanded by standardization. Megan and Rhonda, introduced in chapter 1, are but two examples. Of course, sometimes it is a matter of well-funded and gifted educators working with really gifted children. But often it is good teachers working with ordinary children in different ways.

While the standard model can be significantly improved (as evidenced by the ongoing success of countries such as Singapore and the Netherlands on international comparisons, and by the enormous variation between states in the United States), standardization is not the way to do it. In fact, when ordinary kids can perform at extraordinary levels on a regular basis when taught in ways that are not in accord with the standard model, it suggests that what education—public and private—accepts from kids and the standard model is actually a relatively low level of functioning. Increments of a few points on standardized tests are not really significant when compared with what is possible and should be accomplished across the board.

Indeed, we contend that the standard model is inherently incapable of producing the really high standards that are needed for effective education in the new millennium. Something much more powerful is required. And something much more powerful is possible. The shape that it takes begins to become visible when we look again at how the brain actually learns.

CHAPTER 3

The Natural Learning That
the Standard Model Ignores

The Brain is wider than the Sky
For, put them side by side
The one the other will contain
with ease, and You beside.

Emily Dickinson, *The Complete Poems* (1924)

Our economic survival hinges on a revolution in the ailing educa-
tion system. (Henderson, 2000)

People and machines are different. People are alive and machines are
dead (though some people who are trying to create artificial life may
dispute this fact). Almost every human being has one prime directive
that is a foundation for all others—it is the drive to stay alive. So we
eat, drink, seek shelter, connect with others, and have an immune system that protects us against disease and infection.

And we learn.

The core, central, incontrovertible, essential fact is that learning is a
biological process that we must have in order to stay alive. We resort to
flight or flight when necessary. The fight or flight response is our
body's primitive, automatic, inborn response that prepares the body to
"fight" or "flee" from perceived attack, harm, or threat to its survival.
But even more basic, and more important than fight or flight as the basis for survival, is learning.

We were not born with the capacity to learn in order to get a job, earn
money, go to school, become a celebrity, play ball, found a mega-
corporation, or run for office. These are all things we can do because
we can learn, and because they may be ways that help us thrive and stay
alive. But learning itself is much more basic. Learning is the bridge

between instinct and reality. Learning is what makes it possible to both consciously and unconsciously adapt and adjust to a changing world. It was going on way before schools were invented or direct instruction was thought of. It is what every child in every classroom is naturally doing every second of the day. It is the ongoing, natural process that we must understand first in order to come to grips with what education can and should be.

We will see that natural learning is not the same thing as memorizing rules in math or the dates of various wars. In fact, most systems of training and education have just about forgotten how natural learning works, and so they rely on some very limited natural capacities (like memorization) but totally overlook everything else that is going on in a student's world.

So what is going on?

LIVING SYSTEMS LEARN FOR THEIR OWN BENEFIT

> Every living thing acts to develop and preserve itself. Identity is the filter that every organism or system uses to make sense of the world. New information, new relationships, changing environments—all are interpreted through a sense of self. This tendency toward self-creation is so strong that it creates a seeming paradox. An organism will change to maintain its identity. (Wheatley & Kellner-Rogers, 1998, p. 14)

Let's begin with a peculiar question: what does the immune system do? The function of the immune system is to determine when a virus or bacterium is a "foreign substance" invading the body, so that the body's forces can be mobilized to attack the intruder. For this to happen, the immune system must have a sense of self—it must know whether something is me or not-me.

Each person is an integrated living system. We are not just lots of bits and pieces of muscles, tissues, blood, and brain regions each with a separate function. In addition to that, the body, brain, and mind of each person forms a complete unity.

In this unity, everything is interconnected to everything else and everything influences everything else in multiple ways. The neuroscientist Antonio Damasio (1994) spells this out more formally:

> (1) The human brain and the rest of the body constitute an indissociable organism, . . .; (2) The organism interacts with the environment as an en-

semble: the interaction is neither of the body alone nor of the brain alone; (pp. xvi–xvii)

So every child is, in fact, a "whole" child, surviving by adapting to its world, and it does that by learning. But what does that learning look like? Over the last 12 years we have integrated findings from many disciplines, ranging from cognitive psychology to brain research, into a series of 12 principles of learning for educators that we list in chapter 6. Here we would like to introduce some of the core findings about how people learn. They will clarify standard model misconceptions, and will force even those who care about education to radically rethink most attempts at reform.

MAKING SENSE OF EXPERIENCE: FINDING PATTERNS THAT CONNECT

Jimmy is growing his first garden. He digs up a bit of the back yard, and he makes rows with the toe of his shoe. Then he opens a little packet of beans that his mother bought him and puts them all in the same row. Next he covers up all the rows and then he gets a hose and soaks the entire bed until it is overflowing. Then he runs off to play somewhere else. He forgets the garden for the next few days, but when his mother reminds him that plants need water, he rushes off to get the hose, turns it on as powerfully as he can, and blasts everything in the garden unmercifully. Then he turns the hose off and goes back to inspect the garden. Seeing no plants of any kind, he calls out. "Mummy, mummy. When will my beans grow?" (G. Caine, R. Caine, & S. Crowell, 1999)

Jimmy knows some facts, and probably understands a little about several issues. For instance, he knows that seeds need to be put in soil and watered. But he does not know how or when to water, nor about the impact of water pressure, nor how long it takes for plants to grow. His ideas and beliefs need to be challenged and expanded. As his knowledge and understanding grow, he will have much more success with his plants. In effect, he will grasp the patterns of what works.

A pattern is what Fritjof Capra (1997) calls "an ordered configuration of relationships." In other words, a set or combination of things that seem to fit together. Whenever we try to figure out what something means, we search for patterns that make sense to us. The great anthropologist Gregory Bateson called them "patterns that connect."

We are biologically equipped at birth with many basic capacities for perception that reflect the way the world is and operates. These include the ability to detect lines and edges and curves and movement, light and dark, up and down, basic smells and tastes, loud and soft, and a basic sense of number. Infants are intrinsically attuned to voices and faces and people. We all naturally connect items (like dots or lines) that are close together into a perceived whole. And with experience, the basic elements that we perceive naturally (they are sometimes called natural categories) combine and gel into more complex categories (such as forests and computers and houses and cars) and ways of behaving (sometimes called scripts or schema or maps).

Human beings have added capacities to organize information: we can represent things symbolically where a sign stands for something else, a capacity that is at the heart of writing and math and art. And we can organized things in terms of how they relate to each other, which we do through the use of concepts and ideas. Those ideas and concepts that shape the ways we actually respond to events in life are sometimes called mental models.

Over time, richer and more complex clusters of patterns can take shape in our minds. Some have to do with the story of humans through time (the essence of history), where we have been and where we are located in space (the essence of geography), and how we communicate (language and the language arts). Thus, the core curriculum is an ongoing organization of patterns of collective experience in any culture. And as information accumulates and life becomes more complex, additional and different ways of organizing it all develop—and become new subjects and fields of study or the work of new professions and businesses.

The search for patterns lasts throughout life, and it begins at birth. Anyone who has ever lived through the "why" questions of young children or the seemingly endless curiosity of toddlers knows that children are born with a need to touch, smell, observe, listen to, and generally experience and figure out their world.

We seem to have a kind of explanatory drive, like our drive for food or sex. . . . We see this same drive to understand the world in its purest form in children. Human children in the first three years of life are consumed by a desire to explore and experiment with objects. (Gopnik, Meltsoff, & Kuhl, 1999, pp. 85–86)

The key is that children are interacting with their world and are testing experience. The work of developmental psychologists now shows that from a very early age, every single human being is born with the ability and desire to make predictions about the world, to test hypotheses, to work things out, and to makes sense of things. In many ways the approach of infants and young children mirrors the way that scientists work.

> Look beyond the surfaces of the world and try to infer its deepest patterns. We look for the underlying, hidden causes of events. We try to figure out the nature of things. (Gopnik et al., 1999, pp. 85)

This similarity is why researchers Gopnik, Meltzoff, and Kuhl call infants "scientists in the crib."

At the same time as they are figuring things out, children are also expanding their ways of acting in the world. They develop life skills—speaking, walking, socializing, fixing things, planning, hunting, gathering, investing, and so on. And as every parent knows, those skills and behaviors that children feel to be important are naturally repeated, rehearsed, tested, and practiced time and time again.

Of course, central to the development and acquisition of patterns by children is imitation of, and modeling and guidance by, elders, peers, role models, and teachers and coaches and guides. The crucial point is that the most effective guidance occurs within a meaningful context so that it *makes sense* to the person needing to learn. We expand on the scope and range of context in the next chapter and illustrate the contextual nature of guidance in chapters 5 and 6.

THE PHENOMENAL INFLUENCE OF FEELING AND EMOTION

Most teachers and most parents know that every child is a complex weather system of emotions, yet it used to be thought, and most educators believed, that understanding and feeling were very separate. In part this was because, while clinical psychology placed emotion front and center, other branches of psychology that have a significant impact on education largely discounted the role of emotion in thought and action. Nothing could be further from the truth. In recent years, fortunately, brain research has turned conventional psychology on its head. It is now abundantly clear that the whole process of perceiving, thinking, interpreting, and coming to understand anything is driven by emotion (Goleman, 1995; Damasio, 1999). All of the patterns that we perceive and develop are colored by emotion.

One source of the new understanding is the work of neuroscientist Candace Pert (Molecules of Emotion, 1997) and her colleagues. Scientists have known for many years that neurons are the cells in the brain that transmit the signals essential for all human functioning. They also know that chemicals called neurotransmitters carry signals across the gaps—synapses—between neurons and make thought, mood and emotion possible. In the 1980s, Pert and her colleagues discovered that those same neurotransmitters are part of a class of chemicals (called ligands) that are found throughout the body, including the immune system. Every emotion that a person feels is accompanied by a cascade of ligands affecting the way that cells organize themselves. This is why ligands are called "molecules of emotion." Pert further suggests, partly because neurotransmitters are ligands and are found outside the brain, that every thought—without exception—is accompanied by the secretion of some "molecules of emotion." So thinking and feeling are always deeply interconnected. The theme has been explored quite vividly by Antonio Damasio, quoted earlier. He elaborates, "emotion is integral to the processes of reasoning and decision making, for worse and for better" (1999, p. 41).

An excellent way to illustrate this deep interconnection between thought and feeling is through the eyes of metaphor. A metaphor is a tool for understanding. It is a way of using one idea or situation to make sense of another. Here are some examples from linguist George Lakoff (1987) having to do with *anger*. They show how evocative images are and how much our understandings are colored by emotion.

He *lost his cool.*
He's just *letting off steam.*
Don't get *hot under the collar.*

Lakoff and coauthor Mark Johnson, a cognitive psychologist ahead of his time, go on to argue that metaphors cannot be fully understood independently of how they are experienced (1980). That is, the meaning comes from the complex set of responses and connections that are set up, some of which are emotional responses. Metaphors seem to underlie much of our understanding, and the way we interpret any situation or fact is colored by how it affects us emotionally.

People can be more or less emotional, and some people are much more aware of their emotions than others, but every single one of us thinks with our feelings. Highly "rational" military analysts or computer junkies may dispute this, but even they are guided by the way that they feel about the work they are doing and the people and situations in which the work occurs. Emotions impact thinking and learning at many levels and in many ways.

Purpose, Passion, and Motivation

As we have said, everyone is innately motivated to search for meaning, and that search is profoundly emotional. It involves core values and purposes and the questions that drive us, such as "who am I?" and "why am I here?" Why is it that so much of the advice provided in the world of self-help, therapy, management, and human resource development is that purpose and meaning are crucial to peak performance? "Begin with the end in view" is one of author Stephen Covey's seven habits of highly effective people (1989). James Hillman reaches deeper. He writes that "what is lost in so many lives, and what must be recovered: [is] a sense of personal calling, that there is a reason I am alive" (1996, p. 4).

The rigor, persistence, and perseverance of great inventors, thinkers, entrepreneurs, and others is testament to the power of purpose. One example is Andrew Wiles, a mathematician who dedicated seven years of his life to solving Fermat's last theorem—a three-hundred-year-old puzzle (The Proof, 1997). Another is Nobel Prize winning chemist Ahmed H. Zewail who said in an interview that he had a passion to understand fundamental processes, "I love molecules," he said. "I want to understand why do they do what they do" (Cole, 1999).

Emotion lies at the heart of the motivation that children have for learning. However, motivation is often misunderstood because, when it comes to learning, there are simple and complex motivations. If a child is intrinsically interested in math or history, that interest is a gift to the child and the teacher. However, there are always deeper, less obvious motives that every child has. One is simply the drive to connect and belong to a group and find its place in the world. Related to this is the drive to communicate with people who are important—whether friend or foe. And embracing all is the drive to thrive and succeed and survive in whatever world a child finds itself.

In a world where the ideas and skills to be learned are part of everyday life, *children are motivated to master those ideas and skills, irrespective of what those are, simply because they are part of the world to which the children are adapting.* That is one reason why the best predictor of reading success is a family in which reading is a way of life. For the child, learning to read is simply taken for granted as one of the things one learns to do because it is part of the way that their family lives. It, and other processes, are seen to be natural because they fit naturally into the child's world—they are always there peripherally, they are part of the social fabric of life, there is an emotional connection to them. In short, they are part and parcel of a child's lived experience and are deemed by the child to be necessary.

The Discomfort of Confusion and the Thrill of Insight

One of the primary aspects of mastering new concepts is what psychologists call cognitive dissonance (Festinger, 1957). When a person is confronted with two seemingly contradictory phenomena or ideas, both of which seem to be true, the person is thrown into genuine emotional and personal turmoil until the contradiction is resolved. That resolution is usually satisfying and brings with it a strong sense of relief.

"Getting it" really is thrilling. The sheer pleasure and joy of insight is so great that it is intrinsically motivating and keeps people going.

> Like other human drives, that explanatory drive comes equipped with certain emotions: a deeply disturbing dissatisfaction when you can't make sense of things and a distinctive joy when you can." (Gopnik et al., 1999, p. 162)

Thus, the chairman of Procter & Gamble, John Pepper, explains that business needs schools to nourish

> Basic thinking skills, a sense of discovery and the thrill of success. When students experience these, they will certainly want to learn more. (Hirshberg, September 1999, pp. 40, 43)

This is much like the state of flow described by Csikszentmihalyi (1990). His research shows that when a set of conditions are met, experts dealing with problems in their field of expertise experience a sort of pleasure and bliss as they go about their work so that, for them, time really does seem to stand still.

Great scientists in their research, great artists in their creativity, children at their play, all experience aspects of this state. It is sufficiently compelling, often, to replace other basic needs. It is one of the most powerful motivators in the human repertoire.

Paying Attention

The basic decision to simply attend to a person or event or signal is determined by what we feel and how much we are aroused (Parasuraman, R., 1998). When something novel—an unexpected person at a party, perhaps—or in any way interesting attracts our attention, the response is always partly emotional.

Memory

People have emotional memory systems. The joys, pains, uncertainties, and surprises that surface and that can be rekindled are familiar to all. In addition, the strength and intensity of any memory for an event is determined largely by its emotional pull and tug. The standard memory question that researchers ask is: "where were you and what were you doing when President Kennedy was assassinated?" People tend to remember because the event was so vivid and powerful emotionally. It is for this reason that advertisers package so much of their message in stories and scenes that are intended to tug at the heart and kindle basic emotions.

A General Sense of Well Being ("Positive Affect")

Research is now showing that even moderate fluctuations in positive feelings can influence many aspects of everyday functioning. For example, Ashby and others have shown that mild positive affect, of the sort that most people can experience everyday, improves creative problem solving, facilitates recall of neutral and positive material, and systematically changes strategies used in decision-making tasks (Ashby, Isen, & Twiken, 1999). The alternative has also been established. Sadness, uncertainty, fear, and a wide array of negative feelings can adversely impact health and reduce effective performance.

FIGHT OR FLIGHT: THE OTHER SURVIVAL PRINCIPLE

You've been afraid about Ina. But you needn't be. The worst of this kind of shock is that it puts your thinking out of action and hands you over to your emotions. Now just pull yourself together and think! (Wentworth, 1950, p.172)

One of the most powerful of all emotions is fear. When fear takes over, the other survival principle prevails. We fight, freeze or flee. As neuroscientist Robert Sapolsky writes (1998) a zebra that is being chased by a lion across the savannah doesn't have time to stop and taste the grass. The question is what impact the fight or flight response has on learning and on the capacity to learn?

Sapolsky shows that in an emergency, almost all of the body's energy goes toward mobilizing the fight or flight response. Digestion slows down, growth and immunity are inhibited, sexual drive decreases, and while some memory is enhanced, much of our memory and awareness of the world around us diminishes. Thus, people literally lose access to much of their higher order and creative functioning in order to deal with the immediacy of the moment.

Psychologists have been exploring the same phenomenon for decades. Arthur Combs, a great educator and the founder of perceptual psychology, dealt with the issue in the context of what we notice when crisis erupts. He described it as a narrowing of the perceptual field (Combs, Richards, & Richards, 1988). In effect, as we focus intently on the problem, we become less aware of many other things that are happening around us. The bottom line is that, in times of threat and emergency, we lose access to some of our normal capacities. In effect, we become less intelligent.

Of course, different people react differently, and some people are much more capable than others of dealing with threat and crisis. Our own work for the last 15 years has been built, in part, on clarifying the elements of the fight or flight response in order to better assist learners and teachers. The crucial point is that the issue is *not* simply one of threat or fear. Rather, the factor that drives any animal or person into survival mode is threat associated with helplessness and fatigue.

In 1978 a businessman turned educator, Les Hart, coined the word "downshifting" to describe the phenomenon being addressed. We like that word, and in 1991 we refined the definition. We wrote that "'downshifting' is a psychophysiological response to threat associated with a sense of helplessness or fatigue." When people downshift, they revert back to early programmed behaviors and/or to more primitive and instinctive ways of functioning. Of course, there are degrees of helplessness. It is not a matter of black and white. Thus, according to Perry, Bollard, Baker, and Vigilaute (1955), responses range along a continuum beginning with vigilance.

Most people would have no trouble with the research findings described above. The problem is that often the stress response does not stop:

> If you are that zebra running for your life, or that lion sprinting for your meal, your body's physiological response mechanisms are superbly adapted for dealing with such short-term physical emergencies. When we sit around and worry about stressful things, we turn on the same physiological responses—but they are potentially a disaster when provoked chronically. A large body of evidence suggests that stress-related disease emerges, predominantly, out of the fact that we so often activate a physiological system that has evolved for responding to acute physical emergencies, but we turn it on for months on end, worrying about mortgages, relationships, and promotion. (Sapolsky, p. 6)

Health is adversely affected. And so is the capacity to learn. When people experience stress accompanied by helplessness or fatigue, they downshift and the fight or flight response kicks in. This is absolutely essential in some survival conditions. However, downshifting literally locks people out of some of their own capacity for higher-order learning and creativity. So when fight or flight becomes constant—as it often does in constantly stressful environments—many people begin to function continuously at a very low level. Research collated in our book (Caine & Caine, 1994) strongly suggests that in most circumstances, the standard model of instruction in the standard system downshifts both students and educators. (*See* chapter 6). That is, the school system itself often diminishes the capacity of students to learn.

The standard model, remember, imposes goals determined by others, irrespective of what matters to students, within time lines unrelated to optimal functioning, all driven by a set of externally controlled rewards and punishments. This is a superb combination of factors for inducing a sense of helplessness. Consequently, most students are continuously placed in a state of vigilance where they seek to survive by pleasing their teachers and playing the game demanded by the system. Punishing students for making mistakes is not the way to promote the self-sufficiency essential for initiative, creativity, and risk taking.

OVERCOMING HELPLESSNESS

The other side of helplessness is what psychologists call self-efficacy (Bandura, 1992). It is a combination of confidence in one's own capacity to take charge of a situation accompanied by the skill and ability to do it. This is the competence and self-control that is the hallmark and foundation of peak performance. The key for educators is not to promote self-esteem in students (in the sense of just feeling good about oneself) but real achievement based on real effort that allows students to experience competence and feel proficient. The result is both a reduction in the sense of helplessness and the capacity to recognize helplessness and neutralize it.

It transpires that helplessness can be learned, and so can self-efficacy. Learned helplessness develops when a person is placed in multiple situations where he or she has no control over the outcomes—a phenomenon that occurs frequently in the standard model. Self-efficacy can be developed, on the other hand, when a person has repeated experiences of meaningful success. And one key in turning the corner is what educational researcher David Perkins (1995) calls reflective intelligence, a capacity linked to what other psychologists call metacognition or thinking about the way that one thinks. It is a person's ability to monitor his or her own performance, conduct and state of mind, as a prelude to taking charge and improving. In short, learning itself is indispensable for overcoming inappropriate fight or flight reactions.

In a wonderful video called "Why do these kids love school" by producer Dorothy Fadiman (1988) a youngster in seventh grade at a middle school is talking,

> When 10:15 comes around sometimes and math time comes I just get this kind of . . . a reaction of "oh no, it's math. I don't want to do math." But then . . . I say "Ease up. . . There's nothing wrong with it. So go ahead and do your math."

He has grasped the art of examining his own attitude, and changing it. And in so doing, he changes his performance, the quality of his experience, and the quality of his own learning.

While every person is potentially equipped for metacognition, most people do not do it very well. Much of the world of self-help is actually about the wide variety of tools and techniques available to people to take charge of their own thinking and emotions and, therefore, of their own lives.

At the core of self-efficacy, therefore, is the decision to take charge of one's own learning, supported by adequate opportunities to do so.

That is why self-directed learning is such an important ingredient in the guided experience approach to education.

LEARNING BY BECOMING

The standard model treats the stuff to be learned as separate and detached from the person doing the learning. Brain research shows that to be largely wrong. As people learn about the world in meaningful ways, the learning changes them. They are changed psychologically, and they are changed physiologically (Bransford, Brown, & Cocking, 1999). They are literally reshaped and reformed. The continuous nature of change is why many people regard process as being the essence of meaningful learning. We like the phrase "learning by becoming."

The psychological shift has received some attention from researchers. They have shown that what changes is the way that a person perceives and interacts. In fact, Restak (1995) says, the main purpose of the brain is to "make inner representations of reality" (p. 3). As a result of meaningful learning, we see the world differently.

> As the English chemist and philosopher Michael Polanyi puts it, our language, tools, and actions create faculties: " . . . we interiorize these things and make ourselves dwell in them." By dwelling in them, new organs of cognition arise. (Zajonc, 1993, p. 184)

Once a person "gets" a pattern, it sticks. We get the concept. We see how an airport works. We grasp the flow of traffic or the way the stock market works or how to network to win friends and influence people. We also pick up the ways in which our society and culture think. Different people are "at home" in the desert, in mountains, on the sea, in a mall. There are fundamentally different types of music for instance, with difference rhythms and melodies and chords and sounds. What is really strange to one set of ears is beautiful harmony to another. Prejudice works the same way. A prejudice is what psychologist Ellen Langer (1989) calls a "premature cognitive commitment." A person has learned to perceive some aspect of his or her world—say gender or race or way of speaking—and reacts to that perception automatically and strongly.

As a person learns, the very wiring in the brain changes as neurons connect with each other. Where patterns stick, a myriad of brain cells—

neurons—will fire together in what are called neural networks. The mantra is that "cells that fire together wire together" (LeDoux, 1996). A single stimulus can subsequently set the entire assembly firing together. These networks become the hidden building blocks that house the patterns that constitute our understanding and mental models of the world. They are the basic forms and structures for all the stuff that needs to be recognized and understood.

The Brain Is Plastic

So we now know that ordinary, everyday learning actually impacts the physical nature of the brain. This capacity of the brain to change in response to experience is called plasticity.

Some of the earliest research was begun 30 years ago with rats. Pioneers such as Marion Diamond (1988) and current researchers such as Bill Greenough at the University of Illinois have compared the brains of rats from impoverished and enriched environments. The striking finding is that rats kept in enriched environments tend to have more synaptic connections (links between neurons) and more and thicker glial cells (which are the cells that help to nourish neurons).

What, then, is the difference between those environments. One aspect of an enriched environment is the opportunity for rats to play with toys and items that change every day, as contrasted with rats kept in unchanging cages. Other aspects of an enriched environment for rats includes socializing with other rats, and being touched and stroked by researchers every day. Impoverished environments were, essentially, sensory deprivation and isolation chambers.

Of interest to those of us who have been out of the cradle for many decades, the research also shows a similar difference for elderly rats which, it turns out, can also learn from experience. Though the brain is much more plastic in the early years of life, every single human brain retains some plasticity no matter how old.

One reason why habits are so difficult to dislodge is that we literally have to rewire and reconfigure the body and brain for new habits—it is *much* more than just changing our minds.

Actually, the body changes in other ways in the course of learning. The flow of chemicals in the body, tone of muscles, focus of attention, patterns of breathing, and more shift. Indeed, the entire physiology is engaged in the course of learning, which is why it is appropriate to talk about teaching the whole child.

The practical consequence is that even in a class on math or history or art or computing, we are teaching the whole child. Every facet of their personality—whether they are shy or extroverted, physically adept or clumsy—will come into play and be influenced in every classroom in every lesson to some extent. Each student is interpreting—often unconsciously—multiple aspects of every single lesson and moment in school in terms of what has to be done in order to maintain a sense of his or her own identity. Also being shaped are their beliefs about their own abilities and capacities. These beliefs are powerful predictors for future learning.

And because every person has a unique combination of genes and experiences, every student is unique. They have different sets of genes, different experiences, different interests, different rates of development, different opportunities, different learning and perceptual styles and preferences, different families. Some from stimulating, safe, and secure environments may need less structure in their schooling; some from deprived backgrounds or who are more stressed may need more structured environments. The sad problem of standardization is not that standardized practices are always wrong; rather it is that some practices that work well with some children are being applied universally, to the detriment of countless other children.

IMPLICATION: EDUCATION MUST CAPITALIZE ON THE BRAIN'S NATURAL CAPACITY TO LEARN FROM EXPERIENCE

We all inhabit a world driven by two survival principles. One is to learn how the world works so that we can be effective in it. The other is to fight, or run and hide, when circumstances get out of control. The indispensable core function of education must be to help children learn how to be effective in the world. And the incontrovertible essence of such learning is being better and better equipped to make sense of experience. Education, then, should be society's way to help people expand their capacity to function effectively in the real world.

Children are not machines, so meaningful learning is partly structured and partly messy and disorganized. Because all people are emotional beings, because even when people are in similar situations their experiences are different, because all are uniquely endowed with styles and preferences and indiosyncracies, all people grow their inner representations of reality in their own way and at their own pace. Of course there are many similar patterns of development and growth. Nevertheless, the individual variation in each human being is enormous. The standard model has seized on the alikeness; it pays minimal attention to how to deal with the diversity of uniqueness. The standard model also focuses on the transmission of information; it has almost no grasp of the importance of a child's interaction with life as a basis for making sense of information.

One of the hallmarks of great teachers is that they can vary a general approach in order to accommodate the enormous differences that exist from child to child. However, it is only in flexible environments that such high-level teaching can be effective.

As a way of setting the stage for translating all these points into good teaching and effective education, we suggest that there are three fundamental elements that emerge out of the findings discussed in this chapter. They are interactive and nonsequential, because they all influence each other and often occur simultaneously (Caine & Caine, 1994). Together they constitute the essence of the guided-experience approach to learning and teaching.

An optimal state of mind in the learner and teacher that we call relaxed alertness. This state of mind is a combination of low threat and high challenge. Students need to feel safe enough to take risks and make mistakes. They also need to want to learn, so motivation must be partly intrinsic (from within the person) as well as partly extrinsic (based on stimulation generated by some other person or group).

Orchestrated immersion of the learner in experience in which curriculum is deeply and richly embedded. Orchestration embraces both direct instruction and presentations and engagement by the student in long-term, open-ended projects and events. There will always be some direct modeling and coaching by someone who knows what it's all about, and cares about the learner and the learning. There will also be student-directed exploration of often puzzling experiences as the student grasps for the patterns that connect. That is why content—both concepts and skills—needs to be embedded in ongoing and understandable apprenticeships and projects or experience of some type.

Active processing of the experience by the learner, guided by teachers, so that the content and meanings begin to make sense and take shape in the minds of learners. Active processing ranges from systematic practice and creative rehearsal to the deeply probing and ongoing questions that test the limits of a learner's abilities to think and respond within a real life context.

Rather than expand on these three elements now, we will meet them again in various guises in later chapters. The task now is to identify more of the features of context and experience that must be taken into consideration, and to clarify the differences in knowledge gained from guided experience supplemented by instruction, and knowledge gained purely from direct instruction.

CHAPTER 4

Experience-Based Learning Generates Dynamic Performance Knowledge

A story is told of Barbara McClintock, the Nobel winning American biologist who was a pioneer in the study of the structure and functioning of genes. Her field of exploration was ears of corn.

Another scientist named Evelyn Fox Keller came along when McClintock was in her early eighties and said, "I would like to write your intellectual biography, your story as a scientist. Tell me," she said. "how do you do great science?"

McClintock—who was one of the most precise empirical observers and one of the most rigorously logical thinkers in American science—thought for a moment and said, "About the only thing I can tell you about the doing of science is that you somehow have to have a feeling for the organism." (Palmer in Glazer, 1999, p. 23)

After failing to take into consideration how and why people learn, the single biggest problem bedeviling attempts to improve education is a profound misconception about what it means to actually know something (an issue philosophers have been exploring for centuries). Schooling has gone off the rails because it tends to equate knowledge *about* the world with direct knowledge *of* the world. The standard model as generally practiced promotes the former—lived experience develops the latter. As mentioned in chapter 1, we call the former *static or surface knowledge*; we call the latter *dynamic or performance* knowledge. The problem with the standard model is that it has been devoted to chasing shadows. *Experience of* is not the same as *knowing about.*

The misguided nature of the standard model can be illustrated with three different ways of looking at historical events, such as the story of the American presidency from 1992 to 2000.

THE TRIVIAL PURSUIT
OR JEOPARDY WAY—SURFACE KNOWLEDGE

Anyone surfing the Web, watching television, reading magazines, or even doing serious research can find an inexhaustible number of facts about the Clinton Presidency. Personal facts (name, age, religion, family, state of origin, meeting his wife at Yale); political events (Governor of Arkansas, campaign slogan—"it's the economy, stupid," advisors, policies); personal problems (finances, scandals, conflicts, impeachment). All of this information can be used to answer questions and anyone who can answer a lot of questions will seem to know a lot about the period in question. Yet none of this information by itself would equip a person to analyze the impact of the Clinton years, let alone actually conduct a political campaign. *This type of information is surface or static knowledge. It consists of facts that can be remembered, some of the information that is doubling every two years.*

THE PROBLEM SOLVING OR MIND
GAMES WAY—TECHNICAL OR SCHOLASTIC KNOWLEDGE

All of the information described above has found or can find its way into books, college courses, television talk shows, opinion pieces, political debates, and so on. People can argue about why the presidency took the form that it did, what the causes were for the personal problems that President Clinton had and why the two political parties were so at odds.

Theories, ideas, opinions, assessments, explanations abound. On the basis of this type of thinking people can give advice, analyze problems, propose solutions, and generally seem to make sense of what transpired. Using researcher Howard Gardner's term, we call this *technical or scholastic knowledge.* There is a substantial amount of power in intellectually understanding processes and events. Indeed, a person with this degree of understanding may actually be able to contribute to a political campaign. But a person with this sort of knowledge is most unlikely to deeply understand or conduct a campaign successfully. Something is missing.

THE FELT MEANING WAY—PERFORMANCE KNOWLEDGE

The people who conduct presidential campaigns well or deeply understand them have all the above and more. They have a quality that transforms all the knowledge listed above. They have a *feel* for politics. President Clinton is universally acknowledged to have been a superb campaigner. He had a feel for the process. And that means that he had more than "book learning." All the facts and ideas about politics had been reorganized in his own mind so that he could see the patterns working themselves out as they happened (except, of course, for some disastrous personal mistakes). The knowledge that has become active and real in the world is always accompanied by a "felt sense." It is sometimes called grounded knowing. This is the knowledge that is the gateway to real power because it is the knowledge that is indispensable for effective action. *It is the type of knowledge that can only be gained from real experience. It is dynamic or performance knowledge. Peculiarly, and often unknown to the people who most highly value it, high-level thinking and abstract ideas also become dynamic in the same way, that is, through use in life.*

Let us look, now, at how performance knowledge develops, and the place to begin is with memory.

MEMORY

What does memory mean to you?
It's my story. When I was young and walking to school, I used to take pictures in my mind of what I saw. I even made the "click" sound. I believed I was storing photos for when I was older. . . . that I would be able to peruse them. It's just being able to access my own story.
How do you feel about memorizing facts?
Memorizing facts? That feels disconnected. It feels like outside of myself. It doesn't have a lot of meaning. It isn't really part of my story . . . feels imposed.
What about learning stuff at work?
I do that out of necessity. More times than not I discover what works . . . through discovery I know what works. And even when someone helps me when I'm in a quandary, it feels like a discovery. (Part of an interview we conducted)

Memory has been intensively researched for at least a century. It is known that there are several different memory systems, though there is a substantial amount of disagreement as to what they actually are (See e.g. Squire & Kandel, 1999). Scientists talk about declarative memory (for facts) that can be verbally described, procedural memory (for skills), semantic memory (for meanings), episodic memory (for events), explicit memory (for what can be intentionally recalled), implicit memory (for memory that cannot be intentionally recalled), emotional memory (for emotions that can recur), and more.

For the purposes of education, a very good way to begin is to divide all the systems into at least two different types that overlap. One is rote memory; the other is our natural memory of everyday life events. The central failing of the standard model is that is has been obsessed with the former, and has almost totally ignored the latter.

The best original source of information that we have found comes from the work of O'Keefe and Nadel (1978) who distinguished between what they called taxon and locale memory. Taxon comes from "taxonomies" and refers largely to memorization of facts and skills. Locale comes from location and locale memory refers to our ongoing, spatial, autobiographical memory. It is the natural processes of registering everyday experience.

Taxon or Rote Memory

Everyone is equipped with the ability to memorize stuff that does not yet make sense, and all of us sometimes need to remember facts and procedures before those facts and procedures are really useful. This is how the multiplication tables used to be taught. This type of memory serves two extremely useful purposes. First, sometimes the things learned are essential for survival. A child may not understand much about traffic, but it better "learn" to look left and right before crossing a street in order to avoid being hit by an oncoming car. Second, this type of memory is a sort of way station. Memorization makes it possible for stuff to be learned that will ultimately be understood or mastered. Medical students memorize the bones of a skeleton, for example, long before most of them develop a feel for how the skeleton and the body really work. It is the sort of memory that is used to store the information that we describe above as surface knowledge.

Cognitive scientists have adopted the "information processing" or computer model to explain how static memory is mostly formed (Woolfolk, 1993). Of all the possible information available, some is admitted into short-term memory where it is processed and worked on. With enough work, the information lodges in long-term memory. This is roughly like the difference between ram (the short-term memory on a computer that is used by any software program) and the hard drive (where information is stored even after the computer has been turned off). And, of course, this model is also partly accurate. With enough practice and rehearsal, facts and skills can be memorized and stored for a very long time. This type of memorization can be motivated by externally imposed rewards or punishments, and is at the heart of programming people. All of this confirms that people can "store" items to be called upon at a later date. However the memories are largely unchanging and stay the same in different contexts. One of the most ancient and yet least understood parts of the brain, the cerebellum, seems to be uniquely engaged in this type of memorization (Schmahmann, 1997).

Locale or Autobiographical Memory

Something crucial is missing from the picture painted above. For instance: Computers do not get excited or stressed. Computers do not adapt to the world so much that they change their own operating systems. Computers do not interpret information to suit themselves.

As was pointed out in the preceding chapter, computers are dead. Living systems are constantly adapting and adjusting and, at times, changing their internal models of how the world works. In addition, human beings are connecting all the information and making the changes in order to keep an ongoing record or story of who they are. Here memory is also at work. It is through memory that a sense of self is sustained. So memory is actually the ongoing, changing, internal model or map that a person has of his or her life. It consists of all those patterns (described in the preceding chapter) that have been developed that act as filters and lenses for perceiving and understanding and interpreting the world. It shifts and changes as a person reorganizes his or her internal maps of life.

One of the most powerful and least understood aspects of locale memory is that the internal maps that we all have are partly organized on the basis of concepts and ideas! (O'Keefe & Nadel, 1978). A concept is essentially a way of integrating facts and information. The more powerful the ideas and concepts that we have, the greater the capacity to absorb, integrate, organize, and synthesize information—and so make sense of experience. That is why the curriculum should always make categories and concepts primary and facts secondary.

Static and Dynamic Memory

We define rote memory as *static* because it does not change easily. It consists of facts and routes and routines that remain the same, no matter when we use them. Locale memory is *dynamic* because it is constantly changing.

In the real world the two types of memory interconnect quite naturally. In fact many of our rote memories can become dynamic memories in the course of experience. This happens with a doctor who, as a student memorizes the parts of the body and then, when in practice, begins to see many patients and how their bodies function in different ways. One thing that happens over time, and with plenty of experience, is that the doctor begins to get a *feel* for how bodies actually work.

THE FEELING OF KNOWING

The feeling of knowing is generated when all the processes that we have described work together in some way—thought, emotion, senses, and body. It is as though we come to know something with our whole body and mind. We relate to it or resonate with it. It no longer feels alien but somehow connected. We get it "in our belly."

Some psychologists who have known about this feeling of knowing were far ahead of their time. One, Eugene Gendlin, the former head of the department of psychology at the University of Chicago, coined the terms "felt meaning" and "felt sense" in the context of therapy. Gendlin developed a practice in the 1960s that he called focusing (1981). He argued that much of what we actually believe and think is present in our bodies, often as feelings and sensations that we simply do not grasp consciously and cannot put into words. The goal of focusing is to bring awareness to bear on a bodily state. Very often there bursts forth a sudden knowing, an insight into what had been troubling a person that had been present but invisible. Gendlin calls this explosion of insight a "felt meaning." The identical phrase was used by author and noted management consultant Peter Vail in his book "Learning as a Way of Being" (1996). There Vail specifically invites people who wish to understand something in depth to get a felt meaning for it. More recently, neuroscientist Damasio (1999) has attempted to shed light on what occurs in the brain as people get "a feeling for what happens."

The feeling of knowing can be found in the sports pages in every newspaper. In story after story, in sports as diverse as baseball, cricket, the many footballs, snooker, golf, tennis, and basketball, we hear about the need to have a feel for the game. An example: Peerless Price (real name) was a rookie wide receiver for the Buffalo Bills football team. Speaking of his potential, then-Bill's quarterback Doug Flutie said:

> "He [Peerless] seems to have a real good feel for the game.". . . Flutie points to a play in Washington in which he was flushed out of the pocket and tried to find a receiver as he fled for the right sideline. Price broke off his pattern and Flutie found him for a 17-yard gain. "That showed a lot of savvy," Flutie says. (Brady, 1999)

This refrain runs through much of science, including the molecular genetics of which McClintock was a part. This new science was defined by Sydney Brenner as "the search for explanations of the behavior of living things in terms of the molecules that compose them" (Weiner, 1999, p. 62). It was "a hybrid science, then," continues Weiner, "requiring *a feel* for the behavior of living things, *a feel* for the behavior of matter, and what Crick called 'the hubris of the physicist.'" In a similar vein, a page on the World Wide Web (www.chembio . . . see bibliography) describes some of the early thinking of the great physicists Neils Bohr and Prince Louis de Broglie. It deals with the way in which de Broglie came to the conclusion that elementary particles, like photons, also operated as waves. The story teller concludes

> de Broglie's leap of faith was in asserting that this same expression [for light] should apply to particles. It is instructive to get a *feel* for the wavelength of various particles you might encounter. (emphasis added)

The feeling of knowing extends into other aspects of our lives. Michael Schrage makes the point that great design is certainly not something that comes out of the mouth of a business school professor. Great design isn't taught; it's felt" (Schrage, 1989). While we contest the notion that it cannot be taught, we agree whole heartedly with the notion that what is learned is a "sense." The quality of knowledge has shifted.

It has become dynamic. It it is on its way to becoming useful in life.

THE POWER OF CONTEXT

Why is it that a feeling for something can only come from experience? The answer is that experience provides additional sources of information that are essential to help the pattern to gel. In traditional education, partly because of the shortcomings of behavioral psychology (of which educators made great use), those additional layers of information have never been understood and therefore have never been missed. However, those extra layers are crucial. Collectively they could be called the power of context.

Context provides indispensable input and stimulation for the grasp of any complex idea or skill. Many children surround themselves with pictures and paraphernalia of great athletes and celebrities. Budding artists visit art galleries; budding entrepreneurs surf the Web and often set up small businesses while at school. The context always teaches. A sterile classroom or school is one of the worst possible environments for helping children to learn.

Peripheral Perception

It turns out that one of the marvelous capacities of every single human being is the capacity to relate to and perceive different aspects of the context, even when not paying direct attention to it.

Some of the evidence for the impact of what is not quite seen comes in the form of implicit memory (Schacter, 1996). Let us say that you are in a room full of items. After you leave the room, you might not be able to consciously recollect everything that was there, and you might even swear that some named items were not there. And yet research shows that if experimenters give you the option to identify different items from a list, you are likely to choose those that were actually in the room, even if you never remember seeing them! Guy Claxton calls this learning by osmosis (1997, p. 20).

Commercials work in this way. Even if you see something only once or out of the corner of your eye, and argue vehemently that you did not see the name of the product, given a number of choices in a store you are likely to select or prefer the product you claim never to have seen. That is why advertisers position their advertisements in the context of programs that stimulate identifiable desires and fears in selected audiences. Diane Halpern (1989) tells of a conversation she once had with a cab driver. She and the driver had been discussing the way in which laundry products are advertised on television. The cab driver insisted that he never paid any attention to such advertising and that he always just got the blue bottle that got out the "ring around the collar." Halpern goes on to say, "Although he believed that he was not allowing the advertising claims to influence him, in fact, they were directly determining his buying habits" (1989).

All people move through life engaged in this ongoing dance between attention and peripheral perception. And all are powerfully influenced by signals and stimuli from the environment that are perceived and that color and create a context for whatever is focused on.

> Though many Americans may be hard put to tell you the name of their senator or the country's leading painters or novelists, anyone who is even moderately informed knows the names of dozens of TV actors, rock stars, athletes, fashion advisors and many others who will someday be answers to trivia questions. You acquire this information. (Neal Gabler, 3/12/2000)

The bottom line is that people always pick up impressions from their environment and always make sense of things in context. People vary as to how context sensitive they are, but the opinions that are formed about how the world works and how to adapt are *always* context dependent to some extent.

The key, in teaching, is to make sure that the context supports the content. That is why kids learning to play ball go to ball games, why it is a good idea for an aspiring guitar player to hang out with really good guitar players, why the way to learn about political campaigns is to actively participate in many of them. The sounds, the action, the smells, the sights, the colors, the relationships all help to make sense of the basic ideas and skills. They make the content real and give the learner a feel for the subject.

The Brain/Mind Is Social

One of the most powerful aspects of context is the social setting and the social relationships that develop. Some of the indispensable elements of felt meaning come from the way in which people work together and relate.

A crucial aspect of one's context is the society of which one is a part. Throughout our lives, our brains/minds change in response to our engagement with others, so much so that individuals must always be seen as integral parts of larger social systems.

> We are an intensely social species, deeply dependent on one another for our very survival. (Gopnik et al., 1999, p. 23)

Part of our identity depends on establishing community and finding ways to belong. It has been called the "contact urge" (Brothers, 1997, p. 75).

Imitation is an innate mechanism for learning from adults, a culture instinct. (Gopnik et al., 1999, p. 168)

Even one-month old babies imitate facial expressions. Researchers have shown this systematically by showing a person sticking out a tongue or opening his or her mouth. Babies' faces were videotaped while this was happening. The videotaped faces were then shown to someone else who had no idea what the baby had seen. The second person had to ascertain whether the baby was sticking out its tongue or opening its mouth—and did so accurately and predictably (Gopnik et al., p. 29).

Lev Vygotsky (1978) suggested that even the ability for people to engage in internal dialogue—to think in their minds—is learned after experiencing external dialogue with others.

This interaction between people is very subtle and much of it is nonverbal. In their attempts to explain this connection, some scientists speak of a "mental state resonance" (Siegel, 1999, p. 70) when people are in a form of alignment. This is very important in therapy, for instance.

Such an alignment permits a nonverbal form of communication to the patient that she is being "understood" in the deepest sense. . . . She is "feeling felt" by another person. This attunement of states forms the nonverbal basis of collaborative, contingent communication. (Siegel, p. 70)

The same state assists good parenting and good teaching.

It seems as though the capacity for this alignment is also built into our bodies and brains.

Recently, the neuropsychologist Giacomo Rizzolatti has found neurons in monkeys that fire both when the monkey carries out certain specific hand motions, and when it views those specific motions being carried out by someone else. . . . Based on preliminary data, it is likely that mirror neurons will also be found for other gestures, including facial movements. (Brothers, 1997, p. 79).

The existence of "mirror neurons" indicates that we are biologically built to respond to what others in our environment do. No matter how much a person might like to think of himself or herself as a loner, everyone is designed to imitate and model others. The bottom line is that

Some neurons respond preferentially and selectively to social aspects of our world. (Brothers, p. 37)

The result is that everything that anyone learns is colored by social relationships and the groups of which they are a part. A child learns from its siblings, its parents, and its peers. Mothers of young infants learn from other mothers of old and young infants. A person stepping into any world for the first time—stock brokering, hospitals, road maintenance, outdoor adventure, tagging and making graffiti, journalism, politics, border hopping—all are influenced by the habits and practices and language and values of those in the same arena.

In addition to imitating and learning from others, something even more subtle happens. Collectively, people co-create their ideas and beliefs. These are often the things that "everyone knows." When you and I have an experience, part of the way one of us responds and interprets what happens depends on how the other responds and reacts. Mob hysteria is an extreme example, where a group of people decide that someone is guilty of something and decide to lynch him, without any evidence. The term that is used to describe this phenomenon is "the social construction of knowledge."

Because the brain/mind is social, one's ideas and perceptions are always shaped in some ways by the ideas and perceptions of other people. That is why corporations work so hard to establish their own corporate culture. It is the culture that shapes the way an employee perceives and reacts to his or her work. And that is a further reason why establishing good community is the indispensable foundation for developing better schools. The closer a school comes to being an apprentice community, the more can it capitalize on all the ways in which adults and children learn from and teach each other. Some of the great programs for teaching reading work in precisely this way. They set out to create a culture of reading, a culture similar to that found in those homes that develop in young children a readiness to read.

PERFORMANCE KNOWLEDGE

We now have enough understanding of the brain and mind to clarify the nature of learning in a way that education can use.

In the real world, dynamic memory is primary, and static memory is secondary. When a person is engaged in some meaningful task or situation, dynamic memory is activated. When there is a sufficient amount of interaction with the real world, and enough processing of experience and response to meaningful feedback, performance knowledge is the result. Performance knowledge consists of concepts, facts, skills, and so on, internalized in such a way that they can be availed of appropriately and effectively in both planned and unplanned situations.

As a person gains a feel for something and develops performance knowledge, a great deal of new information is also synthesized and memorized naturally, and even rote memorization (which is still important) becomes *much* easier. When we get a feeling for something we relate to it naturally and meaningfully. With that as a foundation, rigorous analysis and intellectual understanding come more easily, and information and skills are remembered more effectively with less effort. Anyone who has a consuming passion or interest or hobby knows this.

Schooling has suffered enormously because the power of dynamic memory has been lost. Dynamic memory is working in every single person in every single waking moment. It is also working in all students in every single moment as they deal with their total ongoing experience. It just gets ignored or suppressed or bypassed by traditional education. In fact students often fight against what is being taught when there is no connection between content and lived experience.

The development of performance knowledge is extraordinarily important because performance knowledge is the secret to so many problems that training and education have faced. For instance:

Motivation of students: Gaining a feel for something is a part of the creative process. The two of us have defined "felt meaning" as "an unarticulated sense of relationship that culminates in the 'aha' of insight" (Caine & Caine, 1994). An insight is a "gestalt"—a coming together of many systems and much past experience into a natural whole. Thus, meaningful learning and creativity are related processes. In each case, a person will be immersed in experience that is awash with information, questions will be formed and reformed, there will tend to be rigorous thinking and playful experiment, there will be periods when the questions are put aside. And in each case there is ultimately an "aha" that accompanies the grasping of a central pattern, an insight that the person has to have privately and intimately in order to really get that "pattern that connects." As we have pointed out, "getting it" really is thrilling. This thrill becomes an enormously powerful key for education. If students can have the opportunity to gain insight on a regular basis, the sheer joy pulls toward more examination of a topic and reduces many of the discipline problems found in schools that emphasize standardization. In effect, one of the primary defects of the standard model is that it is so joyless.

Transfer of learning: There is a perpetual lament that learning often does not transfer to the workplace or to new environments. Why not? The answer stems from the type of knowledge participants have acquired. The distinction between surface knowledge and performance knowledge plays out in the work place even more than in school. When people develop a feel for an idea or skill, and when they work to deepen the feel as well as mastering routines and procedures, an internal perceptual shift takes place. As we show in the previous chapter, people who "get it" have acquired a new way of looking at the world. That means that they can see the problems that they could not see before; they can grasp the needs of the situation. Those who have not made this perceptual shift literally can not read contexts in a fresh way. Their training does not transfer because they were not equipped with the perceptual lenses that are needed to operate in new environments.

Better memory of facts: The felt sense of anything act as a natural whole and a natural organizer of information and responses. Once a person has a feel for an idea or skill or process, detailed memory of the facts and specifics becomes much easier to acquire. That is why education should aim to give students a feel for core ideas and processes rather than to simply emphasize the accumulation of facts. The facts will tend to follow if the feel is established.

The very real, practical implication is that education should be aiming to do more than develop replicable routines and procedures. It should seek to develop in learners a felt knowing for the material at hand. When that is done a bridge is built between education and the real world, a natural bridge that is located within the hearts and minds of learners.

Oh, That It Were That Simple

Unfortunately, as we venture into the murky domain of the feeling of knowing, a host of issues lie in our path because "feeling" is such an imprecise word.

- *What is the difference between the feeling of knowing and an opinion? After all, if feeling is what counts, isn't every opinion equally "right," particularly opinions about which people feel strongly?* No. But the problem is complex. Every belief that shapes how one perceive the world is grounded in feeling. And so bigotry and prejudice are both "felt." The challenge is to blend intellectual rigor with feeling. Thus cognitive psychologist Bruner talks of the "test by affective congruence" (1967). (see bibliography)

- *Aren't we really talking about intuition?* We are and we aren't. The word "feeling" covers a lot of ill-defined territory. In fact it calls us to reconsider the relationship between knowing and intuiting because great advances in science as well as major developments in business and other domains often stem from an apparently unjustified sense or conviction with people successfully "following their own noses" where others feared to tread.

- *A child does not know as much as an adult. How can they both have a felt meaning for anything? Surely there are differences?* Yes there are, and there is a developmental path for learning such that a novice can have a felt meaning for something (say chess or football) at some level and an expert at another level. The quality and depth of their knowing is profoundly different, and yet each can have a degree of felt meaning.

- *Do "feeling" and "emotion" mean the same thing?* No, but the issue is complex and scientists disagree. We have touched on this above. The word "feeling" conveys something larger in the context of this book, because the entire body is also engaged. This takes us back to the nature of humans as living systems and what some cognitive psychologists call embodied learning. Those teachers who claim to teach the whole child are exactly right, and those who advocate having children sit still for 12 years while they absorb what others tell them are severely limiting the brain by disengaging the body. This will turn out to be one of the chief problems of fully on-line schooling.

- *What happens when a feeling turns out to be wrong?* Science, business, and the arts are rampant with stories of competent, proficient experts who have followed their feelings into disasters and dead ends. Having a feeling is not always a guarantee of being on target. This is why systematic and rigorous thought combined with practical experience is critical, as illustrated by the story of Barbara McClintok with whom we began this chapter.

IMPLICATION: THE ENTIRE CONTEXT COUNTS

A decision has to be made about what type or quality of knowledge education should provide. The standard model is geared towards static knowledge though sometimes such knowledge includes partial intellectual understanding, with a surface grasp of essential concepts. However, the goal should always be to aim for dynamic or performance knowledge that is grounded in a deep, visceral feel for what is being studied as the basis for rigorous understanding, and which depends upon the immersion of the learner in appropriate experience.

In chapter 3 we identified three interactive elements that together are the indispensable core of the guided experience approach that leads to the acquisition of performance knowledge. They are relaxed alertness, orchestrated immersion of the learner in complex experience; and the active processing of experience by the learner.

In this chapter we flesh out some crucial aspects of the context within which these three elements need to occur.

First, students need to be in a safe, honest, and challenging community. Ideally, this quality of community occurs in the classroom, school, and larger world. A good learning community occurs when a healthy set of relationships and mutual respect are developed. The result is that ideas can be safely probed, confusion revealed, and skills methodically tested because useful feedback is uncontaminated by threat, power plays, and the fear of punishment.

Second, because the context communicates, learning is enhanced when the physical environment is designed to support whatever is being studied or taught. Every adult who designs a home to suit him or herself knows this. Every business that pays attention to location, color, atmosphere, sound, and other factors in the environment as a way of communicating better with customers knows this. Every politician who makes an address on television, flanked by the flag or other artifacts knows this. It is time that public education learned the same lesson.

The challenge is to align the several elements that we have identified so that they support each other. A critical aspect, as we will see, is that high-level success generally requires really great teaching because teachers tend to be the orchestraters of it all. We begin by providing some real-world examples of where experience-based learning leading to performance knowledge already takes place, facilitated by teachers, guides, and mentors. This will be a foundation for seeing what the education system needs to do, an issue expanded on in depth in chapter 6.

CHAPTER 5

Real-World Examples of Powerful, Experience-Driven Learning

Thus, the task is not so much to see
what no one yet has seen,
but to think what nobody yet has thought
about that which everybody sees.

(Schopenhauer, 1966)

The life of law has not been logic. It has been experience.

(Oliver Wendell Holmes, 1881)

Perhaps the most astonishing aspect of the debate over education is the extent to which people do not see the difference between surface knowledge and performance knowledge, nor do they appreciate the power and relevance of experience in all meaningful learning. The evidence is everywhere — in all our lives and in every culture. Not seeing these is roughly the equivalent of the fish not seeing water, or a politician not appreciating the need to get votes. Our first objective in this chapter, therefore, is to illustrate the ubiquitous nature of experience in the development of performance knowledge, and so to make the invisible visible.

Our second objective is to show that purposeful, successful, experience-based learning involves the alignment of a series of factors. We introduced the three core elements at the conclusion of chapter 3. They are:

Relaxed alertness as a state of mind: The learner needs to be interested and feel relatively safe and willing to take risks.

Orchestrated immersion in complex experience: The material to be mastered is embedded within complex experiences such as projects and events that often take place over extended periods of time.

Active practice and processing of experience: The learner practices skills and systematically examines and gets feedback from experience.

For those elements to be successfully engaged, there must be adequate support and guidance. More specifically, the learner needs:

A *climate* that is conducive to powerful learning.

Guidance from a teacher, coach, or mentor who has some expertise in the field or skill and who guides the learner in the same way as a good master guides a novice or apprentice in the apprenticeship model.

Broad contextual support for the learning, coming both from the wider community and the physical environment.

INVISIBLE MENTAL MODELS CONNECT IT ALL

Of course, not every element is always present for all participants. What matters is that enough of the elements be present and in alignment for powerful learning to occur. There are many individual differences and a wide range of variation in how everything works together. For instance a situation that is exciting and challenging for some may be unpleasant and intimidating to others. Our goal here is to provide general illustrations of how the overall process works in the real world.

The question is: what ties all the elements together? The answer is: mental models of good and bad performance. The underlying patterns that connect are invisible, but everywhere. As organizational consultant Peter Senge writes:

> "Mental Models" are deeply ingrained assumptions, generalizations, or even pictures or images that influence how we understand the world and how we take actions. Very often, we are not consciously aware of our mental models or the effects they have on our behavior. (Senge, 1990, p. 8)

Generally, novices are guided by mentors who know how something works or what it means, and the mentors use their own inner image or model of good or bad performance as the basis for selecting what is important for a novice to know or do next. In order to help the novice become more proficient, both mentor and learner need regular, useful feedback. That feedback is based on performance. The essence of a "high standard" is always the mental model of a high quality performance.

We will see in later chapters that one core defect of the standard model of education, and of attempts at educational reform, is the absence of mental models of high quality performance. Great education, on the other hand, always comes from an appreciation of what great performances look like and how they develop over time.

FIVE REAL-WORLD EXAMPLES OF SUCCESSFUL, EXPERIENCE-BASED LEARNING

Here are five illustrations of real-world learning that also clarify the meaning of high standards. In some, the larger world overlaps with schooling. In all of them the elements mentioned above come into play. One specific point to look for is the extent to which novices have the benefit of guidance from others who know what it's all about—parents, coaches, mentors, co-workers, professionals in the field. Ultimately, they could all be called teachers, and the way that they work will set the stage for understanding the guided-experience approach that is essential for schooling to re-form.

Acquiring One's First Language

From birth (and possibly earlier) everyone begins to acquire his or her native language. All children are born with the inherent capacity to master every one of the more than five thousand languages on the face of the earth. And even if no one teaches a child how to speak, a child learns to do so if simply immersed in the lives of others who speak.

There is a pattern in the development and acquisition of language, elegantly captured in *The Scientist in the Crib* (Gopnik et al., 1999). The foundation is an "implicit set of rules" (p. 99), that is a part of the inheritance of every infant. These are some of the natural categories and patterns that are mentioned in chapter 3. The rules, a type of natural grammar, make it possible to translate sound into meaningful ideas. But translation does not just come automatically. In every infant mind there is a kind of ongoing puzzle: to "find out what the folks around here do and learn how to do it yourself. The other folks are crucial" (p. 101). So language is a social phenomenon, and the infant with its unconscious rules is grappling with the way to use them in the society in which it finds itself.

Where to begin? It turns out that language begins long before infants speak their first words. Every language has a sound system—a rhythm and pattern of sounds and inflections and signals and cadences. In our early months, all of us were potentially able to discern the sound system of every language on the face of the earth. Yet within six months, a particular sound pattern begins to take shape—it is the sound pattern of our native language.

> Why do the speakers of different languages hear and produce sounds so differently? Ears and mouths are the same the world over. What differs is our brains. Exposure to a particular language has altered our brains and shaped our minds, so that we perceive sound differently. This in turn leads speakers of different languages to produce sounds differently. (p. 104)

In fact within the space of one year, babies have proceeded beyond discerning sound patterns to discerning some of the rules that their language has about words, even before they master words themselves. And even their babbling shifts very quickly from a sort of universal way of producing sounds to babbling in a way that sounds like their native language. In one experiment, some French speakers were asked to listen to many babbling babies. They were able to ascertain with almost one hundred percent accuracy which of the babies were French.

In due course words and then sentences begin to emerge out of the babble. The pattern of development is shaped by the babies' culture. For example, Korean children tend to acquire verbs before nouns whereas Western children tend to acquire nouns before verbs.

All this development requires interaction with others. Infants imitate adults (and their siblings). Infants also interact with others in a sort of infant dialogue of "coos" and "ahs." They begin to make sense of words based on other things that have already begun to make sense in their lives. And in every culture of the world they are guided and encouraged and thrilled by "motherese" or parentese.

> Motherese sentences are shorter and simpler than sentences directed at adults. Moreover, grown-ups speaking to babies often repeat the same thing over and over with slight variations. . . . But the clearest evidence that motherese helps babies learn comes from studies of the sounds of motherese. Recent studies show that the well-formed, elongated consonants and vowels of motherese are particularly clear examples of speech sounds. Mothers and other care givers are teachers as well as lovers. (p. 130)

Thus, there is motivation to speak, to connect, to belong in an environment that is safe and that encourages and thrives on risk taking. There is immersion in multiple experiences, some of which simply involve being in the presence of competent speakers, and others of which involve extensive social interaction with people of different linguistic capacities (from other infants to older children to adults). There are developmentally appropriate and natural links with care givers who guide, model, demonstrate, and facilitate the acquisition of language. There is an enormous amount of affirmation of the efforts of the infants, and yet the expectation is that the child will ultimately get the words and grammar right. And there is a great deal of practice, experimentation, trying, and working things out.

The acquisition of language is a superb example of the combination of experience and naturally guided instruction. The primary test is always performance. Every human being passes. And while the language capacities of people do vary substantially, everyone has the natural capacity to master language at a very high level. Of course, all people have innate linguistic abilities, and so there is a biological foundation upon which experience builds. The question is whether the underlying process operates elsewhere as well, and it does. Music provides an example.

Suzuki Method for Teaching Music

The date is July 11, 2000. The program is the *NewsHour* on the Public Broadcasting System. The setting is Ottawa, Kansas. The story is about a superb music teacher and a town that almost bursts at the seam with youngsters playing the violin. The twist is that many of these children began playing between the ages of two and three. They are performing complex pieces at the age of six. They are playing like prodigies, except for the fact that they are not prodigies. They run the gamut of "ordinary" kids being taught in an exceptional way. Teacher Alice Joy Lewis is using the Suzuki method.

Suzuki felt that if three-year-old Japanese kids could master thousands of words and manipulate chop sticks, they could probably play music very well at an early age. He was right. He developed a process that capitalizes beautifully on what we now know about high-performance learning and teaching. The special features are spelled out by the Suzuki Association of the Americas (www.Suzukiassociation.org). His belief is that musical ability can be acquired in the same way as one's mother tongue, and he modeled that approach intentionally. The essential components follow:

Early Beginning: The early years are crucial in child development, both for mental processes and muscle coordination. As we saw from the research on language acquisition, young children also have extensive aural awareness, and Suzuki felt that this is an excellent time to establish musical sensitivity. He said that listening to music should begin at birth and formal training may begin at age three or four, though it is never too late to begin.

Listening: Just as children learn to speak in an environment filled with language, parents can also make music part of the child's environment. Part of the art is to attend concerts and regularly play recordings of the Suzuki repertoire and other music. This enables children to absorb the language of music just as they absorb the sounds of their mother tongue. By virtue of repeated listening to the pieces they will be learning, children become familiar with them and easily learn to play them.

Parent Involvement: As we show above, parents are important teachers as a child learns to talk. According to Suzuki, parents also have an important role as "home teachers" when a child learns an instrument. In the beginning, one parent often learns to play for a few months before the child begins, so that s/he understands what the child is expected to do. Parent and child listen together to musical pieces; the parent attends the child's lessons; and the two practice daily at home.

Repetition: Suzuki noted that when children have learned a word, they don't discard it but continue to use it while adding new words to their vocabulary. Similarly, Suzuki students repeat the pieces they learn, gradually using the skills they have gained in new and more sophisticated ways as they add to their repertoire. According to Suzuki, the introduction of new technical skills and musical concepts in the context of familiar pieces makes their acquisition much easier.

Encouragement: As with language, each child learns at his/her own rate, building on small steps that can be mastered. This creates an environment of enjoyment for child, parent, and teacher. Support is increased by sincere praise and encouragement.

Learning with Other Children: Suzuki felt that music promotes healthy social interaction, and children are highly motivated by participating in group lessons and performances in addition to their own individual lessons. They enjoy observing other children at all levels—aspiring to the level of more advanced students, sharing challenges with their peers, and appreciating the efforts of those following in their footsteps. Cooperation and generosity of spirit are encouraged in these larger groups.

Graded Repertoire: With the Suzuki method, students learn musical concepts and skills in the context of the music rather than through dry technical exercises. The analogy is to speaking, because children do not practice exercises to learn to speak, but learn by using language for communication and self-expression. The Suzuki repertoire for each instrument presents a careful sequence of building blocks for technical and musical development. (We would advocate more choice than the Suzuki method usually provides.) Suzuki also believes that this standard repertoire provides strong motivation, as younger students want to play music they hear older students play.

Delayed Reading: In the same way, Suzuki students develop basic competence on their instruments before being taught to read music. This was because Suzuki believed that children are taught to read only after their ability to speak has been well established. (This is the other main tenet where we believe he may have been misguided).

Quality: In the development of skill, Suzuki urged both teacher and student to focus on the development of good posture, beautiful tone, accurate intonation, and musical phrasing.

Note that Suzuki believed that music is available to all people. Exceptional capacities are not required. He explicitly and intentionally modeled his process on the developmental aspects of language. And the clear goal is for children to play music—to successfully perform. Our next step is to see if many of the same processes can work in other domains in the later years.

Becoming Proficient in Sport and Athletics

Michael Jordan and Tiger Woods are two of the most recognized figures on the face of the planet. They have in common the fact that they are kings of their respective sport—Jordan probably the best basketball player of all time and Woods on his way to becoming the greatest golfer. Each has inspired dreams in the minds and psyches of young children and adults and each has contributed significantly to the growth of his sport. Other athletes such as gymnasts Nadia Comaneci and Mary Lou Retton have also inspired adoration and emulation. As symbols and celebrities, they are key elements in a much larger and pervasive culture of sport and games.

On Dana Point beach just South of Laguna in Southern California, a young parent throws a large, soft beach ball to his very young daughter. It bounces off her hands and rolls away. She giggles furiously as she pursues it, pushing it further away with each touch. Finally, with a little assistance, she manages to hit it in the general direction of her father, who applauds loudly. They do it again. And again. And again. When he is too tired to go on playing, they retreat to the shade of an umbrella where the family is gathered. Dozens of other families are on the beach, many engaged in very similar activities.

The early steps of motor control and game playing are unfolding. The level of performance is engaging and challenging without being overwhelming. There is relationship and fun aplenty within a supportive family environment. And there is a larger social setting within which all of this is taking place and which shows that the practice is natural.

A young boy is dressed in a football uniform with helmet in hand. Impatiently he waits for his mother to bring the car round to take him to his game. As he rushes off to join his team mates, she joins friends in the single stand at one end of the playing field. Soon the two teams run onto the field. It is a scaled down replica of a major stadium, with the field properly laid out, umpires and whistles, fans (parents) on the sidelines and in the stand, and a score board. The coaches of each team prowl the sideline, talk to and guide the players (and sometimes shout at them), and strive to have the team work together. Some of the unpleasant aspects of sport emerge as well, as some parents abuse the umpire, yell at their kids, and confront each other. After the game the young boy goes home and up to his room where a poster of his favorite professional ball player is on his wall. Later that night the whole family watches television where they see stories of how the professionals did, and perhaps hear about some of the personal stories of their heroes and those they call villains.

Notice, also that all the elements of sport are embedded in and woven into the culture and everyday experience. The social and physical context "teach" many of the aspects of sport constantly. There is now a higher level of coaching and direct instruction. There is some review and analysis after an event and, when appropriate, during the event. The game is a natural part of the life of many families, often a burden, but supported by and carried on in the presence of parents. The game and games generally are featured in the media in multiple ways with scores, stories, and highlights seeping directly and sideways into the consciousness of kids. And all the trappings of praise and blame, triumph and failure, glory and ignominy that play themselves out in the larger arena become aspects of the life of the children who absorb them. Even at school, sport is ubiquitous. The name—"badgers," "eagles," "fighting Trojans"—is emblazoned on a marquee. The week's results are featured. Key players become leaders in the society of students (and, often, of adults). And the status and relationships of many students are defined by the connectedness with sporting events.

Beyond school there is college. Key players, male and female, are recruited heavily. Sport tends to be well financed, and in some institutions is a key to raising money and recruiting nonathletic but highly regarded students. National associations preside over college sport and dealing with them is part of the task of college presidents. The national media feature games between nationally ranked teams. Coaches at major colleges are revered and earn enormous salaries. And the instruction, the practice, and the fitness drills are intense. Direct instruction occurs at an appropriate level, in the context of a deeply involved culture. And much that is mean and cruel and simple minded about the whole affair is also present, as it is in the larger world. Of course, only a minority of students play seriously, but many play socially and follow the serious ones. Sport is everywhere, and all the elements that we mention at the beginning of this chapter are integrated into the learning and teaching of players and athletes.

And so it goes, with the colleges acting as farm clubs for the professionals, whose exploits command national and international attention. Some athletes become so celebrated in fact, that they begin to set the tone for how the culture itself behaves and sees itself.

Note that success is *always* a matter of performance. Some become skillful in playing the sport; some become skillful in reading a game while they played (as Magic Johnson did with basketball and Richie Benaud did with cricket). But even those of us who are not great athletes and yet still love sport interact in a practical, real-time way as we watch games or talk with friends or write columns and do commentaries. Observers and audiences are also exercising a type of performance knowledge.

Interestingly, people who engage in sport and athletics tend to form or join associations, clubs, and networks with similar beliefs and cultures. In all, they participate in communities of practice. The same thing happens at work.

Communities of Practice in the Adult World

People who work together in a common pursuit learn together and teach each other. Where groups function like this in a community pursuing a common enterprise created over time, they are engaged in what social scientist Etienne Wenger calls a community of practice.

In many ways they teach each other directly. For example, Wenger describes people whose job it is to process claims in an insurance company. Here is a part of a meeting that he observed:

> Harriet then asks the processors if they have any items of business to bring up. The assistant-supervisor complains that there have been too many overpayments lately. She blames it on the fact that processors do not check eligibility carefully enough. Nancy reminds everyone that they cannot keep paying for physical therapy for a long time, even with a new prescription from a doctor. They must have a progress report. And if physical therapy goes on for more than a year, it has to be referred to the technical unit. Finally, Beliza says, "Well, for me, it's just this deductible." Everyone understands what she is talking about. Certain plans stipulate a complicated way of determining when a family deductible is satisfied. An animated discussion ensues with everyone contributing examples and partial explanations until Beliza seems satisfied: "It's easy to explain here, but it's a pain to explain it on the phone." she says. Many processors nod. (Wenger, 1999, p. 26)

All the elements that we have identified are present as the workers learn together. They have a job to do. Some love the job; for others it is simply a way to earn a living. In all cases, it is personally important to the participants—to Harriet and Beliza and the others—that they understand what the work entails and how to do it.

In that context, they have been given some training by the company. They have been introduced to their job, shown forms and how to fill them out, introduced to the requirements that must be followed and so on. But it is totally clear that experienced processors know many other things. For instance, they "do not fill out their forms completely; they wait until they have completed the entire claim" (p. 30). And as is evident from the meeting described above, they all share insights with each other, and those with experience help others to understand what is happening.

Look, next, to the social relationships. Over time a common language has emerged, so that they all understand the phrase "Well, for me, it's just this deductible." As Wenger describes the workers in more detail, we find that there are common concerns; they share stories together; birthdays happen; there are groups and subgroups; a real society is developing with many taken-for-granteds and beliefs and subtle ways of behaving.

This entire mode of functioning as people learn with and from each other plays out again and again in other groups with common practices. Philosopher and scientist Thomas Kuhn points out that

> Every scientist serves an apprenticeship, at school, university, and during graduate research, during which he or she picks up, in a largely unconscious way, certain ways of thinking and approaching knowledge. (Peat, 1996, p. 41–42)

Here, for instance, is a description of Woods Hole, a center of scientific activity in the Northeast United States. Just as children acquire their native language, so the language of science becomes second nature to scientists.

> Woods Hole could never be mistaken for one of the many other summer resorts that dot Cape Cod . . . It's the scientists themselves who give Woods Hole its unmistakable air. Whether waiting for the drawbridge that bisects the town to be lowered or for a bowl of chowder in a local restaurant, they are in constant conversation. Their scientific jargon— "ATP" "calcium spikes," "symbiotic bacteria"—always fills the air, mingling at the beach with the lapping of the waves or in a restaurant with the smells of coffee and fried clams. (Allport, 1986)

In every one of these communities, the participants are dynamically interacting with each other. Some may be novices, some expert; some office workers, some researchers. But in every real-time, real-world interaction the knowledge that is called on is knowledge that guides performance, because even a reaction or response to some other person or to a situation involves a performance.

Interestingly, a similar dynamic atmosphere can be conjured up quite naturally when business and schooling are purposefully aligned to enhance the learning.

Learning Science and Math through School/Industry Partnerships

From April 10 to 12, 1997, several thousand students and adults crowded into several arenas at the EPCOT Center in Orlando. They had gathered to participate in or observe the competition for the best robot in the United States. Robots driven by students were competing against each other in the gentle art of stuffing basket balls into a net while seeking to prevent the opposition from doing the same thing. The atmosphere was genuinely electric. The noise exceeded expected decibel levels. The competition was thrilling. And the competitors? They were teams of high school students partnered by professional engineers from major corporations throughout the United States.

The program, under the auspices of an organization named FIRST (formerly USFIRST), had been conceived and developed by Dean Kaman, a very successful inventor and entrepreneur, in order to boost math and science skills in the United States. Kaman had the advantage of not being an educator. He was free to adopt a model and process that might not be politically correct. And that is what he did. Kaman decided to model his robotic competition on football, with a culminating event modeled on the Superbowl—the game that determines what Americans immodestly call the world champion.

Corporations were invited to sponsor teams from any high school interested in participating. At a precise moment in March each year, each team would receive the same type and quantity of parts. A spending limit of a few hundred dollars would be set. And in a six-week period, the students and engineers working together would design and build their robot. While the format remains the same, the task set for each robot varies significantly from year to year. Materials include 12-volt batteries, aluminum, fiberglass, plywood, PVC pipe, structural foam, pumps, air cylinders and valves, and a programmable control system. Each robot can weigh up to 120 pounds and must fit inside a 3' x 3' x 4' space.

A total of 155 teams competed in the 1997 FIRST Robotics Competition. Teams included: AT&T/Texas Instruments and South Brunswick High School; 3-Dimensional Services and Oakland Technical Center; Baxter Healthcare Corporation/Northwestern University and Johnsburg High School; and NASA Ames Research Center and Woodside High School. Over 200 teams participated in 1999, and more than 400 in 2000. In fact the competition is now so large that there are several regional events every year that produce those who enter the "nationals."

Individual comments tell part of the story: "I like it—the fact that you just start with nothing and you create something functional and you get to work with NASA engineers," said Jeff Puente, a senior (Shedden, 3/5/99).

Anne Buchanan, a launch site support engineer for Boeing and the team's mentor, says she's amazed by the relationship she and the students have developed. "You get to work with students on a more equal footing, though you're still mentoring them," she said (Shedden, 3/5/1999).
Different types of results tell more of the story.

> There are literally hundreds of examples of students completely changing their attitudes about education and their scholastic performance. Principals of inner city and lower performing schools are beginning to tell stories of incredible turn arounds in entire schools. In one case, East Tech High School in Cleveland, Ohio, passing grades in state proficiency tests have gone from 43 to 71 percent since the inception of the FIRST program there. Working with engineers from the NASA Lewis Research Center, this school and team have created an intense demand for technical activity. More students there try out for the first team than basketball and football combined! (Shedden, 3/5/1999)

The corporations involved are also benefiting. They have begun to use the process as part of their own training. In addition to being invigorating and stimulating for the adults, opportunities are provided for adults to develop more creativity, improve prototyping skills, improve relationships, and function more effectively with time constraints.

Note again that, when all the elements mentioned at the beginning of this chapter work together coherently, an extraordinary amount of effective learning takes place in many domains and on many skills simultaneously. In the FIRST program there is an apprenticeship model embedded in a largely supportive social setting. Expert engineers work with students to codesign robots using state-of-the-art math and science, in a context endorsed by teachers, parents, and peers. Rather than students simply following from behind, they tend to be engaged and coached in "real time." And the scoring system in the competition reflects real-world performance in a genuinely exciting setting. The entire program then sets the stage for math and science becoming more meaningful in school, and so more people attend classes—even traditional classes. More students are dynamically engaged in subject matter mastery. And better results on orthodox tests follow.

The program has now expanded dramatically. We write above about high school students. However, there is now a lego league for youngsters, with equally promising results. (Visit them on line at www.First.com).

A word of caution is in order; we are not unquestioningly endorsing the competitive sports model, and there may well be groups in the population who tend to be or feel excluded. The point is simply that the approach adopted is very powerful because it implements the factors that together lead to powerful learning.

The Rest of Us

There are some good models of combined instruction and experience within schools. They include the school-based apprenticeships of some musicians and artists. On occasion, talented people and prodigies have the opportunity to go to schools that are geared toward developing their talent and skill. The Juilliard School for Music and the Arts in New York is one such college. The Idyllwild School of the Arts in Idyllwild, California, is, in many respects, one such high school. For these few, the world of experience is infused in a systematic way into their education. Ordinary education sometimes seeks to accomplish a similar goal with magnet schools, which tend to be public schools based on a theme or focus area such as the arts or technology.

Such schooling did not happen that way for most of us. We were instructed in class but we gained our experience outside the traditional classroom, either after the school day or our school years ended. The sport model does not stand alone. Much the same set of phenomena occurs in politics. Kids run for class president, emulating their elders with their speeches and promises. Some become volunteers in campaigns, manage campaigns, and end up running for office or being involved in politics in other ways.

The beliefs and values that permeate society tend to be transmitted in the same way. The indispensable core element of the dynamic or performance knowledge that kids acquire comes from the world with which they interact. Kids emulate adults and other kids. Kids are exposed to the media and other sources of messages and signals about what is right and what is wrong, but the consolidation of what is cool and what is not emerges out of their interactions with peers, parents, and others.

To the extent that the system of public education has worked adequately in the past, it is because the pace of change for society as a whole has been relatively slow. Most of us have had time to move into the after-school world and slowly become proficient at our work as we gain more life experience. Some of us had hobbies in which we indulged outside school or in some specific courses. Photography, making movies, scuba diving, writing poetry, acting, taking cars apart and rebuilding them. These often became the center of our postschool careers and framed the skills and knowledge that we acquired.

The exponential increase in the amount of information facing all of us, and the accelerating pace of change means that the gap between schooling and life experience is becoming more of a fatal gap. Study and lived experience need to be integrated in school for all children, just as they are in the examples described above. For that to happen, the culture as a whole needs to see what is important. Perhaps most important of all is the type of testing and assessment that is used. And the indispensable key is performance assessment.

IMPLICATION: GOOD PERFORMANCE DEPENDS ON USING PERFORMANCE ASSESSMENT WELL

All learning is developmental, and one aspect of development is the progress from novice to expert. In the examples in this chapter, infants are guided in language acquisition by people who speak well, the young violinists were taught by an expert, the students in the robot competition worked with very proficient engineers, the athletes were coached by people who knew the sport, the workers in the insurance company learned from those who already knew the ropes.

The teachers (the people who acted as coaches, mentors, and guides) were competent practioners. These people had a mental model of what success looked like, and most had a mental model of the developmental path necessary for learners to become competent. Proficiency occurred by approximation as learners took some steps, received feedback, and attempted to do things better.

In essence, successful learning in all the examples described above was revealed by how a learner performed. So, in every case, learner and teacher needed and used performance assessment.

Of course, there are many facets of performance, ranging from state of mind to the contexts in which proficiency is expected. Successful assessment therefore depends on identifying appropriate indicators as well as on occasional precise measurement. A successful sprinter, for example, needs motivation and good technique in order to run the time that is ultimately measured. Here is a way to begin.

Motivation and Involvement

Ideally, students should be "hooked on learning." Intrinsic motivation is a key to high standards simply because it means that students will tend to persist and practice and respond to feedback without being forced to do so. Here are some indicators of intrinsic motivation to look for. They apply to all the learners in the examples presented in this chapter.

Do learners pursue a topic or skill on their own?

Do learners persevere voluntarily, even if the work is difficult?

Do learners enthusiastically talk about the issues they are investigating or the skills they are acquiring?

Do learners find their own resources and look for answers beyond the material given?

Are learners excited by the insights and results they have?

Do learners willingly experiment or take risks with an idea or process to accomplish their own goals or just to see what happens?

Is attendance high without the use of punishments and rewards?

When answered in the affirmative, these reveal passion, interest, intrinsic motivation, commitment. The infant learning to speak, the child shooting hoops for hours every day, the hobbyist immersing him or her self in journals and discussions, the employee taking extra courses or asking for help. Of course, sometimes people just pretend to be motivated and often there is a mix of intrinsic motivation and extrinsic pressure. But over time, their behaviors will show whether interest and motivation are real or not. The behaviors will also help a teacher or coach to see what aspects of an issue or skill a learner is most interested in, and provide information for intelligent guidance.

Real-World Performance

Stages of development and degrees of competence are revealed in the real world all the time. In the cartoon "a family circus," one child points to a convertible car and says, "There's a car without a lid!" His grasp of some concepts and confusion about others is absolutely clear. A person playing his first game of football gets the ball and starts running toward his own goal. The coach immediately sees how little of the concept of the game has been grasped. A young violinist plays a melody exquisitely for the first time. The teacher knows and acknowledges. All of these are real-world signs of how proficient a person is, and all provide the basis by means of which a teacher or coach can guide a learner forward.

The more subtle but equally important task is to recognize real world situations. Here are some indicators that we use:

The ability to use the language of a discipline or subject in social interaction;

The ability to perform appropriately in unanticipated situations;

The ability of learners to ask their own pertinent questions;

The ability to solve real problems using the skills and concepts;

The ability to show, explain, or teach an idea or skill to another who has a real interest or need to know.

Of course, some indicators reveal more than others about different students. We consider them as frames of reference—guides for what to look for as mentors help people acquire performance knowledge.

The peculiar inadequacy of education and the standard model is the failure to grasp that real-world performance is at the heart of academic success as well. High standards are not revealed primarily in the answers that a student gives on a standardized test, but on whether a student can use concepts and procedures in complex, real-world situations. The core goal of education should be to develop students who:

Can think mathematically, not just answer math questions.

Can think historically, not just know some historical facts.

Can do science, not just answer some facts about science.

And just as infants begin to acquire language from birth, and children learn to play a sport at a very early age, so can every aspect of the core curriculum and every subject and field of study deemed to be important, be taught for real-world proficiency from the very beginning. All of the factors that we have identifical in this chapter need to operate in school. Great education does just that, as we see in the next chapters.

CHAPTER 6

What Great Schooling Looks Like

In such a classroom, students play an active role in decisions, teachers work with students rather than doing things to them, and the learners' interests and questions drive much of the curriculum. The environment supports children's desire to find out about things, facilitates the process of discovery, and in general meets children's needs. A school with this mission has a climate very different from one in which educators are mostly thinking about how they can make students work harder or follow directions. (Kohn, 1998, p. 277)

In chapter 5 we introduced a set of features that need to be in alignment for powerful learning to take place, and we provided real-world illustrations of where this already happens. Here we would like to go further, and show high-standard schooling that gets it right. We will describe some success stories that together blend the private and the public, the personal and the business, early learners and later years. In some ways the examples look different, but they share some fundamentals that are absolutely critical for the emerging future.

In all of the examples the indispensable core is the combination of three elements that we introduced in chapter 3 that together comprise the guided experience approach to instruction: an optimal state of mind for learning that we call relaxed alertness; the orchestrated immersion of the learner in experiences in which standards and the curriculum are embedded; and the active processing of experience by the learner, guided by teachers, so that real learning takes place. In all the examples, the students are very successful on tests (where tests are administered) and also acquire an exceptional foundation of dynamic, performance knowledge.

In order to ensure that the three elements are implemented effectively, they need to be aligned with some other critical elements.

- A good understanding by adults in charge of how meaningful learning occurs.
- Clear, high standards framed in terms of mental models of high-quality performance.
- A good sense of community and relationship in the school and classrooms.
- Performance assessment as primary with standardized assessment added.
- Widespread social support and a supportive physical environment.
- A system of management that supports the process.
- Great teachers who are at home with an apprenticeship model.

FOUR STORIES

The four stories told here cover the gamut of education from early childhood to the end of secondary school. We do not deal with college and university, but should add that the more advanced levels of the best graduate schools actually implement the practices and processes that we discuss. We should also add that the two of us have worked with and introduced our ideas and processes to the staffs of two of the four places described below, the Arthur Andersen Community Learning Center in California and Tahatai Coast School in New Zealand. Some of the environments are more advanced than others in the extent to which they function as apprentice communities. In all of them a guided-experience approach to learning and teaching prevails.

Reggio Emilia (Early Childhood)

Within a few days after the end of the Second World War, a group of people in the Emilia Romagna region of Northern Italy decided that they needed a school for young children. They had no money (though they thought they might be able to sell a used tank to raise funds). A field had been donated by a farmer. They planned to use material from bombed houses and elsewhere, and would look for resources where they found them.

The founders wanted the schooling to be public, but an additional challenge, the opposite of that experienced in the United States, is that Italy is a Catholic country. All education was deemed to be an affair of the church, and secular education was almost impossible to fund. Thus it was only in 1963 that city funds for a secular school became available. And now? The city of Reggio Emilia, with a population of 130,000 people, has a municipal early childhood system that has become recognized and acclaimed as one of the best systems of education in the world. Currently the city finances and operates 22 preprimary schools for children aged 3–6, as well as 13 infant-toddler centers for children aged 0–3 (Edwards, Gandini, & Forman, 1996).

The story is told in the book *The Hundred Languages of Children* and in a continually changing art exhibit that tours the United States.

> Because the system grew out of a parent cooperative movement, there has been from the beginning an explicit recognition of the relationship or partnership among parents, educators, and children. Classrooms are organized to support a highly collaborative problem-solving approach to learning. Other important features are the use of small groups in project learning, the teacher/child continuity (two co-teachers work with the same class group for three years), and the community based management method of governance. In Reggio Emilia, education is seen as a communal activity and a sharing of culture through joint exploration between children and adults who together open topics to speculation and discussion. (p. 5)

The environments are flexible and delightful. For instance, each contains an art center and places where children can be alone or together.

The children explore their environment and express themselves through many "languages." These include words, movement, drawing, painting, sculpture, shadow play, collage, and music. Thus art is not simply a subject that is "taught." Rather, the arts are media of communication and learning and teaching. While the means may be different, everyone is geared toward helping children express their own thinking and process their experiences symbolically. Thus, there is a very clear, high-order goal—symbolic representation—but the rest of the curriculum emerges as appropriate from the projects of the children. It turns out that, although very young children are linguistically limited, they have much greater conceptual and representational capacities than have been believed. They can use art to actually reflect on their own thinking, problem solving, and processing.

And they have superb results, generating this comment from Lilian Katz an American academic who has observed and worked with the system.

> It seems to me, then, that a first lesson from Reggio Emilia practices is that pre-primary school children can communicate their ideas, feelings, understandings, imaginings, and observations through visual representation much earlier than most U.S. early childhood educators typically assume. The representations the children create with such impressive skill can serve as a basis for hypotheses, discussions and arguments, often leading to further observations and fresh representations. Using this approach we can see how children's minds can be engaged in a variety of ways in the quest for deeper understanding of the familiar world around them. (p. 25)

The Arthur Anderson Community Learning Center (Secondary School)

Creative Learning Systems is a business located a few miles northeast of San Diego. The vision of the founders was to create a powerful high-tech learning environment that could be implemented in today's schools. In their promotional material they say:

> A Creative Learning Plaza is a large open environment for up to 150 people, working together. . . . In this environment, everyone is a learner and both young people and adults can be facilitators. . . . [in] the interior landscape . . . the furniture is reconfigurable, the reference materials are delivered on demand through networked interactive multimedia, and the place is constantly buzzing with activity.

There is provision for videotaping on location, capacity to simulate physical- and computer-generated models of real-world projects and use of concept mapping software. Works of art can be downloaded, software is available to assist in literary text analysis, and provision is made for intimate small group discussion.

One of the first plazas to be established was a school within a school in Encinal High School in Alameda County near Oakland, California. It is called the Arthur Andersen Community Learning Center, having been funded by Arthur Andersen in the early years. The plaza accommodates 150 students, from grades 7 through 12. They spend every day on site, though some subjects such as physical education are taken in the larger school. The only criterion for admission is that parents apply, and if too many wish their children to attend, decisions are made by lottery.

Students of different ages and in different grades work together on complex projects, utilizing the resources of the facility. For example, on one occasion the selected experience had students use pieces of lego supplemented by electronics to build a model of the Mars rover. Teams designed rovers to suit their imagination. Only when the rovers were completed did the facilitator ask, "Well, what can they do?" At that point the rovers were placed in a simulated environment and the real testing and active processing began—for speed, control, resistance, friction, and the like. With results in hand, students could then rethink, redesign, and retest their rovers. In this way some of the core subjects of the physics curriculum were dealt with in a practical and yet very high-order way.

The school has participated for two years in the robotic competition created by USFIRST (*See* chapter 5). It has honors students who take subjects such as physics and biology at college level, with assignments based on authentic research of questions to which the answers have not previously been found. The daily schedule is fluid so that there are both intensive, planned seminars in subjects such as math, as well as open periods for as long as a day, for perhaps two or three days some weeks, in which students can work on really complex projects.

Results are excellent, based on the products and performance of students. In the only comparison that we know of on California Stat 9 and district standardized tests, the students in the school performed higher than the other high schools in the district. The plaza does pay a price for its philosophy on standardized tests. The facilitators do not cover some material that will be tested but which, in their opinion, the students are unlikely to ever use. Consequently, even though students may have a very good grounding in, say math, they will be unfamiliar with some topics that are tested and so their test scores will suffer. That is a difficult decision to make in the current climate, but it is undoubtedly correct.

Tahatai Coast School (K–6)

New Zealand has created 23 contracts for model elementary schools whose mission it is to have the best possible education program with information technology at its core. Tahatai Coast School, whose foundations were only poured in 1995, is one of those lead schools. It was designed by a local architect to take into account the local environment and was the first New Zealand school to be established under its own Board of Trustees. This gave the school enormous flexibility and choice with the approval of plans, appointment of staff, and the purchase of resources.

The school is richly organized around technology. It has complete broad-band Internet access through a dedicated ISDN line connected to an ISDN Router. Every school computer has access to Internet and email. Each staff member has their own school e-mail address and every class has two addresses for student use. They state:

> We do not purchase or use ready-made pieces of software which simply allow children to "sit and click," rather we allow children to experience and use highly sophisticated multimedia authoring software, video editing, graphic design, Web Authoring and Presentation, publishing and word processing, 3D graphics, and databases. Software examples are mounted on the school's file server and evaluated by staff and students. We are not constrained by using only so-called "educational software." Rather, we expect our students to use the same tools as the professionals would use. (www.tachatai.school.nz/aboutus/aboutus.html, p. 7)

Many classes are multiage and multigrade. Much of the curriculum and instruction is project based. In part because of the combination of European and Maori traditions, art is emphasized nearly as much as technology. And the school devotes considerable resources every year to staff development, always grounded in leading edge theories and research about the nature of learning and teaching, and with a view to developing a learning culture and learning community.

The students successfully participate in national and international competitions; the faculty write and mentor educators from around the world; and in 1998 Tahatai was one winner of the Apple school-of-the-year awards for the way in which it integrated technology into education. For a taste of what they are like, visit them at www.tahatai.school.nz.

Homeschooling

When we wrote our book, *Making Connections: Teaching and the Human Brain*, we included a headline that appeared in the *Los Angeles Times* on December 31, 1987: "3rd Home-Taught Youth Off to Harvard." The paper told the story of Reed Colfax, one of four brothers who were taught exclusively on a family ranch in Boonville in Mendocino County, California. Of the three who had been admitted to Harvard to date (the fourth was only 12), their first formal test was the Scholastic Aptitude Test for college entrance. The entire curriculum involved immersion in experience with ongoing performance assessment. For instance, they learned algebra and geometry as they and their parents built a house, and science, including genetics and embryology, while raising livestock.

They also used textbooks, buying several on any one subject and then as a family deciding which they liked most. "When we started out here, we did hard physical work outside, or we did schoolwork, so schoolwork was always a break for us," said Reed, a long-distance runner, jazz enthusiast, and guitarist. Another son, Drew, also spoke. "I think the four of us know more about the anatomy of an animal than anyone at Harvard . . . I just had a white rat dissection lab that was so boring. It was 'Here's the stomach and here's the heart'."

The sons are not geniuses, according to their father. Rather they are highly motivated and enjoy learning. He also believes that it is the methods themselves that are important because Reed, who is black, and Garth, an Eskimo, were adopted. Their parents were, however, also well equipped. Miki, the boys' mother, is a former high school English and creative writing teacher, and David, their father, has a doctorate in sociology from the University of Chicago. "'When Grant [the first son] was accepted, the story was bumpkin goes to Harvard,' said David Colfax, who served on the Mendocino County school board. 'Now the hook on the whole story is what are we doing right. . . . It raises a lot of questions about education in America . . .'" (*Los Angeles Times,* 12/31/87, p. 21).

The Colfaxes have also written a book—*Home Schooling for Excellence* (1988). Our delight lies in seeing an approach that meshes perfectly with the other examples we describe. It is the approach—the way of understanding and thinking—that is indispensable.

WHAT THE PROGRAMS HAVE IN COMMON

Some are high tech, some low tech. One works with infants through six year olds, another with K–6, another with adolescents, and one ran the gamut of ages. One is in a country with constitutional separation of church and state; another is in a Catholic country where secular education has been very late in coming. They are very different. And yet they are very much alike.

Understanding by Adults Involved
of How Meaningful Learning Works

There will never be effective change in education unless adults in the system appreciate what is actually happening in the brain and mind of children as they learn. Similarly, parents will not support change unless they understand what is involved and what is being done with their children. It is therefore essential to introduce a common set of ideas and a common vocabulary that can form the basis for a shared philosophy of learning. The adults in all four enterprises have a set of shared beliefs and a core theory in common (though they may use different terms). In recent years the approach has come to be called "constructivist" because the underlying theme is that meaningful learning occurs as students make sense of their own experience or "construct" meanings. The key, for us, is not just that students gain intellectual understanding, but that schooling helps students construct or develop useful mental models of how the world works.

Our approach has been to frame the ideas expressed in chapters 3 and 4 of this book in terms of a set of 12 learning principles. They were first published in our book *Making Connections: Teaching and the Human Brain* (1991, 1994), and have since been modified as our own understanding has grown. Those with a background in the area will see that our principles incorporate research from many fields including cognitive psychology, stress theory, work on multiple intelligences and individual differences, developmental psychology, and more. Our method was to use the burgeoning field of brain research to provide a systematic framework for many ideas and research findings.

We present the principles in the form of a wheel, to illustrate that they all operate simultaneously. From one point of view the principles are very simple. They are designed to make some obvious sense when first read, but to act as a gateway to the enormous body of research and experience that has accumulated about learning in the course of the last century. The wheel in this diagram can be downloaded from our Web site, www.Cainelearning.com, as can one chapter of our book *Mindshifts* (1999) which expands on the principles in somewhat more depth.

One example of the use of these principles can be found in the "Learning to Learn" project being implemented by the Department of Education in South Australia. A consortium of about 70 schools has embarked on a multiyear endeavor, and our principles are being used as part of the common intellectual foundation for the effort (www.sacsa.sa.edu).

The Caine Brain/Mind Learning Principles

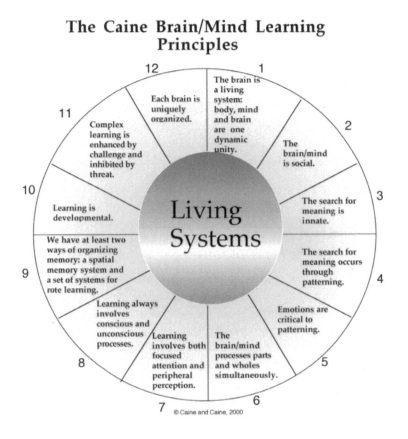

12 — Each brain is uniquely organized.

11 — Complex learning is enhanced by challenge and inhibited by threat.

1 — The brain is a living system: body, mind and brain are one dynamic unity.

2 — The brain/mind is social.

10 — Learning is developmental.

Living Systems

3 — The search for meaning is innate.

9 — We have at least two ways of organizing memory: a spatial memory system and a set of systems for rote learning.

4 — The search for meaning occurs through patterning.

8 — Learning always involves conscious and unconscious processes.

7 — Learning involves both focused attention and peripheral perception.

6 — The brain/mind processes parts and wholes simultaneously.

5 — Emotions are critical to patterning.

© Caine and Caine, 2000

Clear, High Standards

All of the schools have very high standards. All of them, just as in the standard model, spell out some essential skills and knowledge that students need. The indispensable additional core is that the teachers and facilitators are proficient in what they teach, and have an internal mental model or representation of how their subjects and disciplines play out in life. Their standards are always partly framed in terms of what high-quality performance looks like, and of what can be expected from novices and more advanced learners over time.

From the perspective of this dynamic inner world, the educators frame their daily and monthly objectives in a very different way from the standard model. Rather than spell out specific sets of facts and skills and then target them one by one, the educators in these examples keep all the specific standards in mind, but teach in such a way that results tend to emerge "naturally." Thus, the facilitator in the Mars Rover exercise at the Alameda Center knew exactly what principles of physics needed to be taught. He knew what questions to ask, what aspects of design to focus on, and what students needed to grasp. But he also knew that the various insights might occur at unpredictable moments as students conducted their experiments. His job was to keep tabs on what was being learned and to ensure that the prescribed "standards" were addressed.

A Challenging and Safe Community
in the School and in the Classrooms

Students need to feel safe and to feel and allow themselves to be challenged. For that state of mind to be sustained overtime, a good climate and sense of community in the school as a whole, and in classrooms, is vital. The climate begins with the adults, including staff and teachers employed by the school and the children's parents. In this regard, the attitude of the adults in Reggio Emilia, and of the Colfaxes, is exemplary.

In the other two schools, Tahatai and Alameda, community building among the adults is an intentional and systematic process. Community is more than being civil or "nice" to each other. For teachers, an atmosphere must be created which invites, encourages, and allows professionals to also acknowledge what they do not know and to take significant risks as they learn more.

For example, at the Alameda Plaza, teachers hold what they call "deep discussions days." Every two weeks or so the five facilitators gather, and one will present an idea or teaching approach that he or she has been working on. In a climate they universally describe as safe, the five then examine and critique the presentation, provide feedback, discuss the implications, and generally reflect on their understandings of learning, teaching, and professional development. Tahatai has a similar philosophy, and commits substantial resources to professional development. In 1999 we were invited to supplement their other practices by introducing our own *Mindshifts* small group process, and our work with the school continues.

Building community is vital, but not easy. Here is a comment from Cindy Tucker, the principal of a small Title One elementary school where we first tested our process many years ago.

> At this point, we're in the process of becoming a learning community. Our study groups are meeting regularly, and, after some adjustments and refinements, everyone has a home. There are layers upon layers of feelings, some interesting conversations, questions and comments, insights and connections. I think we're right on track with the change process as we experience a mixture of exhilaration, exhaustion, determination, uncertainty, reluctance and passion. (personal communication)

What is little understood is that the climate created in the school is reflected in classrooms, and as teachers begin to respect each other and grasp the importance of their own ongoing learning, they find it much easier to understand and implement the sort of learning climate that is present in really great classrooms.

A Guided-Experience Approach to Instruction

How can a teacher incorporate student interests when students may know nothing about a subject? How can one help a student acquire a "feel" as well as an understanding for a topic or skill? The answers to these questions and others depend on the instructional approach that teachers use.

In all of the examples that we provide, teachers regularly introduce students to new subjects through what we call "global experiences." As much as possible, the global experience needs to touch students emotionally and challenge their thinking. Again, the Mars rover from Alameda is one example. Here is another.

The Colfaxes write:

> And interests emerged, though not necessarily on schedule or in forms parents intend or expect. A visit to the ballet may result in an aversion to, instead of an interest in, dance. And budding artists have been known to prefer baseball to art galleries. But, more typically, days at the zoo may evoke a general interest in wildlife, or a special interest in snakes, or spiders, or bears. Some of these early interests will be mercifully short-lived, while others will persist and expand. (D. Colfax & M. Colfax, 1988, p. 53)

Another example comes from a colleague of ours who used to teach poetry to sixth graders in a traditional didactic way. As she began to understand more about learning, her approach changed. One of her favorite introductory global experiences, now, is to turn her classroom into a simulated coffee house with table cloths on tables and soft music playing. Adults—teachers and parents—are invited to read their own poetry. Then adults and students discuss what they like about poetry and why a poem said what it did or took the form that it did. In this context, almost every child becomes enthused—but they tend not to become enthusiastic about the same things. And so the way is opened for learning about different types of poetry, powered by the students' actual interests.

Note, again, that the teacher keeps the "standards" in mind. She knows what must be covered, but she follows the learner and takes advantage of opportunities, as they arise, to embed prescribed concepts, facts, and skills. She also opens up the learning so that students can pursue issues and topics beyond what have been prescribed. This requires a very high level of expertise, and invariably goes beyond a standardized approach or curriculum. But very good results on standardized tests follow. This particular colleague, for instance, is one of the lead teachers in her district. We should also add that, just like Megan and Rhonda in chapter 1, the heavily prescriptive standardized approach that her district is now pursuing is forcing her to look elsewhere, and may drive her out of teaching altogether.

The Active Processing of Experience
by Learners Guided by Teachers

Perhaps the greatest reason for the failure of many experience-rich approaches to teaching is the lack of appropriate guidance and follow-up. Remember that for a guided-experience approach to succeed, teachers *must* have the standards in mind and know the subject well. With this preparation as a foundation, the task of teachers is to help the students "work" or "massage" the experience to adequately learn from it. Teachers then can ride the wave of student interest by asking questions, providing more material, directing research, and generally helping students gain insight and become skillful. As we mention in earlier chapters, we call this the active processing of experience. Thus, the passage from the Colfaxes quoted above continues:

> It is the parents' task to facilitate the development of these interests to the point that the child can take control and manage activities related to him on his or her own. (p. 53)

The teachers in Reggio Emilia understand perfectly. For instance, on one occasion a group of four and five year olds from "pre-primary schools undertook an extended study of an exceptionally large cooperative supermarket in their neighborhood" (Edwards, 1996 p. 21). They visited the store often, once when it was closed! The shopped there, preparing shopping lists, paying, and using the items to cook when they returned to school. They submitted a "wish list" to the manager, and more. What the teachers found was that

> When the topic of a project is very familiar to the children, they can contribute to the project from their own knowledge, and suggest questions to ask and lines of investigations to pursue; the children themselves can take leadership in planning, can assume responsibilities for specific observations and for information and artifacts to collect. Such projects investigating real phenomena offer children the opportunity to be the "natural anthropologists" they seem born to be! (p. 23)

There is an art to asking questions and guiding thinking. Sometimes the questions will be very basic: "What happened? Why do you think it happened?" Then the questions can be directed: "What would have happened if . . . ? How would such and such influence your opinion?" And always, the teacher keeps the standards in mind.

A superb scenario for educators presented itself with the 2000 Presidential election in the United States. For five weeks after the vote, the decision lay in doubt. The issue was dealt with by several state and federal courts, with the result ultimately being determined on a five to four vote by the U.S. Supreme Court. Meanwhile a host of possibilities were canvassed in the media, and the legislative and executive branches of government in Florida and the nation were engaged. Many members of the press commented on the "civics lesson" we were all getting, and they were right!

A good teacher can use the scenario to teach a great deal about the U.S. Constitution and the separation of powers, the makeup of the Senate,

Congress, and state government, the way the Supreme Court and other courts operate, the way elections run, the pervasive nature of politics and much, much more. All of it can be done through questioning for clarification of facts and logical thinking, guided research, occasional minilectures by the teacher, sharing of results by students with each other, teacher guided discussions and more. And students would master the facts and gain deeper understanding, just as many of us in the larger community, in the United States and much of the rest of the world, learned from the sustained, real-world "civics lesson."

We should add that we are not seeking to throw out the baby with the bath water. There is often room for teachers to lecture, provide information, and use prescriptive practices including rote memory. Even with very sophisticated students there will be times when a teacher just talks, tells, and demonstrates. The difference lies in the reason for using direct instruction and in the purposes and meanings to which students can connect. For example, many students may come from homes where no foundation for a subject has been laid, where children have learned to feel helpless, or where they lack some basic attitudes and skills. In situations such as these one of the most powerful tools in a teacher's kit is a range of practices for giving really interesting presentations and using what we call creative practice and rehearsal.

One of us (Renate) had the opportunity to confront this problem when she taught for one semester in the small charter high school that we helped to create in our village (we tell the story in the next chapter). Many of the students came from fragmented homes, had not done well in other schools, and were, in general, ill-equipped for high-level learning. Some direct instruction worked very well in this environment (Caine, 2000).

Performance Assessment Supplemented by Standardized Tests

The educators in all four places know that real assessment occurs continuously in the process of guiding the learning. Ongoing projects provide automatic opportunities to ask questions, both during and after specific actions. Author and management consultant Donald Schon (1983) calls this reflection-in-action and reflection-on-action. Conversations provide natural opportunities to hear what students actually know. In Reggio Emilia, the "conversations" and "questions" take place in the many "languages" of the arts. But children are very capable of showing their thinking, their conclusions, and their ideas symbolically.

When we asked Mark Beach, the principal of Tahatai, about results, he e-mailed us as follows (November, 2000):

> How do we convince the Ministry, ERO, parents (and ourselves) that children are making progress, especially in thinking and academic ability? We do it through:
> - standardized national tests e.g. TOSCA, PAT, etc.
> - Running Records for reading
> - Records of oral and written language
> - National and school-based standards (Achievement Objectives out of the Curriculum Documents and well as our own School Based Assessment standards)
> - entry in national/international competitions (video, web site, multimedia)
> - Australian Schools' English, Science and Mathematics Competitions
> - School Entry Assessment (all 5 year olds in NZ are tested) and 6 Year Nets (all NZ children at 6 are tested)
> - We believe however that the MOST powerful form of assessment is actually the students' own portfolios (hard copy and digital) where they have ownership of their goals (based on the identified school goals) and manage their learning through development of process and skills

One critical consequence that promoters of standardization seem not to grasp is that, as students taught in the ways described above begin to acquire dynamic knowledge and real skill, their memory of relevant facts and routines and procedures is stimulated. That is why they can automatically being to perform better on standardized tests that tend only to look for the surface knowledge reflected in these memorized materials. The one limitation is that not all material may be covered. In this situation, performance on standardized tests will be adequate (as illustrated by Alameda) but other indicators based on performance and authentic assessment, often from the perspective of acknowledged experts in the field, reveal that powerful, high-level learning is occurring.

Widespread Social Support and a Supportive Physical Environment

All the personnel in these places know that context influences, shapes, molds, and teaches. They all understand the need for a combination of secure, stable places and a great deal of fluidity. They work to ensure that the messages spelled out by the context support what is being taught. The Colfaxes got it right. They noted that

> The child who is exposed to books at an early age, who sees his or her parents reading, who is read to, and who is encouraged to spend time with picture books, will all but certainly become a reader in due course. How and when this occurs will vary from child to child and from family to family. (p. 55)

They go on to describe the very different ages when their four children learned to read, and yet to note that they all became very proficient readers.

The larger environment contributes to the learning as well as the more specific home or school environment. In Italian life, the arts are pervasive. In the learning plazas, the emphasis is on information technology which is also embedded everywhere in the larger world. In Tahatai the sea side environment and the Maori culture are reflected in the design and practices of the school. Moreover, in Tahatai, the arts and technology are very beautifully integrated, in part because they have grasped ways in which to use technology to promote an understanding of design and image. And the Colfaxes lived on a farm with substantial diversity of activities in a rural area of California, with both parents being very well read. In three of the four contexts, the specific intention was to make the environment as delightful as it could be.

A Democratic System of Management That Supports the Process

Each example requires people to pool skills and resources and work effectively together. It requires a common purpose and coherence of action. It is felt by those involved to be in their best interests to work together. And even though there are usually key people in leadership roles, there is a way of working together, sharing ownership, and accepting individual and joint responsibility. None of the four examples described above is laissez-faire, where anything goes. Each uses some traditional management skills and techniques, ranging from record keeping to planning. There are roles and functions, with some people having more power than others. None find the traditional curriculum impossible to navigate. And yet they simply do not function in the normal bureaucratic way.

The key for all of them is a different way of thinking about how to work together. For some it was intuitive; for others it emerged out of deep reflection. The central feature of their approach to management is authentic democracy. This does not necessarily mean that everyone had or has an equal vote in every decision. They all have some elements of a hierarchy. But in each one of them there is genuine respect for everyone else—everyone has a voice and is heard. Students are not permitted to do absolutely anything they like, but their interests are acknowledge and worked with; members of staff actively participate in administrative decisions, and their voices and votes count.

The system works because it has some additional strengths. Although in each there may be a formal chain of management, there is also a great deal of networking—students, parents, staff, outsiders all interact with each other and not simply up and down a hierarchy. Each example capitalizes on the immense power of relationship, and they tend to go out of their way to open up possibilities for people to interact and work together. One practical consequence is that time is organized to suit the learning and teaching, and not fragmented to suit administration. Thus, at the Alameda Plaza, there are some tightly scheduled seminars as well as large blocks of time appropriate for complex problems and projects.

In this type of setting, information and understanding and ideas and suggestions spread like wildfire, and reinforce each other. One science teacher at the Alameda Center called it a "virus" model. But the power of this connectedness depends upon common purposes, common values, a common vision. Thus, people can pursue their own interests and know, in general, that they are simultaneously furthering the interests of the school.

IMPLICATION: THE GUIDED-EXPERIENCE APPROACH IS VERY POWERFUL, YET VERY FRAGILE, AND DEPENDS ON GREAT GUIDES

When the elements that we have described are aligned, very high-level learning occurs for "average" kids. The elements fit together and reinforce each other. For that very reason, when the elements are fragmented or are out of alignment, it is possible to invest a great deal of effort and get nowhere.

The problem is that it is so easy to speak one thing and mean another. It is also possible to sabotage powerful learning and teaching unintentionally. It takes a particular kind of person and a high degree of professionalism to make guided experience work.

As we use the term, a teacher can be a professional educator, a parent, an administrator, a counselor, a nurse, and so on. Whatever their background, and whatever the context, great schooling requires great teachers who can orchestrate experiences, respond to students, react appropriately in unexpected situations, guide learners with information and probing questions, and more. Sometimes a situation does the teaching. Sometimes our peers do the teaching. But any systematic schooling endeavor requires great teachers.

There are, however, enormous differences of opinion about what great teachers look like, and how to help them develop. The problem with the standardization movement is that it almost seeks to make school teacher proof, and the rewards and benefits go, not to those who can cope with complexity but to those who are at home with inflexibility.

Our research (Caine & Caine, 1997) suggests that there is a very clear developmental path for educators. Specifically, while there are many strategies and skills that can be mastered in a routine way, the more complex ways of functioning always depend upon a set of personal qualities as well as a set of skills. For example, it is not possible to create safe community just by practicing some listening skills, though good listening is important. For a person to function well in, and create, a good learning community they must be genuinely interested in others and in sharing ideas with them. Similarly, it is not possible to teach in the way we suggest if a person has very little subject knowledge, or very little grasp of how different subjects connect with each other. On the contrary, really good teachers have a great deal of expertise in some areas that they teach and are also adept at seeing how some idea or issue can be learned from a variety of different experiences.

The problem is that great teachers can be stymied by the system. It seems to us that the standard model uses much of the language used here—"high standards," "powerful learning," "good community," "support for learning"—and yet the dynamics of the standard model systematically prevent powerful learning from taking place on a wide-ranging basis. We examine some of those "limits to growth' in the next chapter.

CHAPTER 7

How "The System" Limits Growth

For almost half a century I have witnessed and have been a participant in efforts generally to improve our educational system. . . . I came to see what should have been obvious; The characteristics, traditions, and organizational dynamics of school systems were more or less lethal obstacles to achieving even modest, narrow goals. (Sarason, 1990)

Many attempts have been made over several decades to reform and improve the standard model. Even most of the elements of experience-based education have been promoted at one time or another since the 1960s. Specific processes that have been attempted range from cooperative learning (a way of grouping students to learn together) to authentic assessment (the use of portfolios of student work and public performances to demonstrate learning). There have been sustained, community-oriented efforts to work with entire schools such as the coalition of essential schools led by Sizer (1997). Some, such as Kovalik and Olsen (1997) have developed comprehensive models of curriculum and instruction.

Results vary enormously. There is absolutely no doubt that the standard model can function more effectively than it does in most of the United States. On the basis of the international comparisons referred to in chapter 2, for instance, students from countries such as Singapore and the Netherlands regularly perform very well. In addition, our observation, confirmed in countless discussions with educators, indicates that it is easier to make changes in elementary schools than in middle or secondary schools. And even improving elementary schools is extraordinarily difficult.

Improvement is difficult because of the lack of alignment between the elements described in chapters 5 and 6. For the most part there are just too many constraints on what can be accomplished, and the limits to growth and restrictions on change are enormous. Unfortunately, the peculiar paradox of the standardization movement is that, in the name of revolutionizing education, it is reinforcing a mind set and a system that actually make it more difficult to deliver the results that are needed.

- In part it is a matter of erroneous beliefs about learning, teaching, and standards.
- In part it is a matter of system constraints that inevitably sabotage experience-based learning and teaching.
- In part it is a matter of power plays that downshift educators so that they become primarily interested in their own survival.

THERE IS NO SUCH THING AS A COMMON STANDARD

A standard refers, among other things, to the flag or symbol under which armies fought. The term "raising the standard" originally meant "raising the flag," whether in an act of defiance or at a moment of victory. It is somewhat ironic, therefore, that the education battles are currently being fought in the name of raising standards.

While the word "standard" is used everywhere that education is in dispute, the word still means different things to different people. The strife in which education finds itself is partly because those different meanings of "standard" reflect different belief systems that are competing with each other, sometimes in open warfare.

Our contention is that the standard model is based on a series of misconceptions about learning, teaching, and assessment, and that standardization is pushing those misconceptions to their limits. The primary misconception has to do with what it means to know anything. To summarize, in general, the standard model and standardization promote the acquisition of static or surface knowledge. In general, the guided-experience approach leads to the acquisition of dynamic or adaptive or performance knowledge. Each has a different type of outcome, each deals with teaching differently, and each has a different approach to assessment. In our view, the guided-experience approach accommodates and includes surface knowledge where necessary, but the standard model has no room for performance knowledge.

The tragic consequence is that the misconceptions about learning, teaching, and assessment incorporated in the standard model and the standardization movement impose a pattern of practice (and support an administrative system) that automatically exclude much of what is essential for high standards of learning to be possible for most students.

Limiting Teaching

The standard model is static. Lessons are planned, issues are chosen, students do assignments in prescribed ways at prescribed times. The guided-experience approach is dynamic. While teachers know what is to be taught, they respond in the moment to what students need. The business world has a term for products that are available on a needs basis. It is "just in time" supply. The guided-experience approach has large components of "just in time" teaching. Standardization so rigidifies the standard model that the dynamics of real learning are impossible to address. This rigidity is particularly prevalent in the early grades and in the teaching of reading and math.

The differences are reflected in different assumptions and practices, such as the following:

Assumption: The sequence for teaching any competence or skill is clear and invariable. It is correct that skills need building blocks so that some systematic development is needed. However, there is enormous variation within any skill, and many possible stepping stones for reaching the same degree of proficiency. Thus, it is appropriate to develop systematic methods (such as the Suzuki method described in chapter 5), but good methods always allow for variation, interaction, and flexibility.

Assumption: Basic skills should be taught before any useful teaching of higher-order competencies is possible. Immersion in a meaning-filled complex environment should occur at the same time as basic skills are taught. Infants may acquire language in a developmental way, but they are immersed in a world of language from birth; artists and scientists need to hone skills over time, but they also dwell in a world of art and science while they are still novices in their practice; children who learn science can acquire high-level observational skills doing art; and learning to read is known to improve abstract thinking.

Assumption: Individual differences in student abilities are so small as to be irrelevant in setting standards, arranging time tables and class schedules, and mandating instructional procedures. Even very bright children can develop at very different rates. Language takes time to develop; good readers can differ by years in the age at which they begin to read; some people only discover "what they want to do when they grow up" after they have grown up.

Assumption: All subjects and skills can and should be taught sepa-rately, irrespective of how much they are part and parcel of each other in the real world. Of course every subject or skill has its own vocabu-lary and set of organizing ideas and processes. However, these are always intertwined with other fields. Projects and other complex experiences work precisely because different subjects and skills are integrated in nat-ural ways. For instance, a well-done project to grow plants and vegeta-bles in an elementary school or an environmental-impact assessment and statement well done, includes science, math, social studies, and the language arts. (*See*, e.g. Ecoliteracy: Mapping the Terrain, Capra, 2000)

The general blindness of those in the system to the enormous vari-ability in human development and to the complexity of good instruc-tion, including the blindness of many who are very proficient in the practice of their own discipline reveals itself in many ways. For exam-ple, an article in the *Los Angeles Times* on November 18, 1999 reported the following:

> Nearly 200 top mathematicians and scientists, including four Nobel Lau-reates, are urging U.S. Secretary of Education Richard W. Riley to with-draw the government's endorsement of math programs that experiment with nontraditional teaching methods. (Colvin, 1999)

This is precisely the same problem and the same old-think of the stan-dardization of practice. Those "nontraditional" methods—when they are done well—are largely intended to combine rigorous skills and rou-tines with experiences that help children make sense of what they are doing. In fact every one of the signatories to the letter experienced those "nontraditional" methods in graduate research. We argue that the graduate model is simply a version of a good model that works best at every age. Guided experience relies, for example, on student research of topics that are personally interesting, and yet make it possible for the "basics" to be covered and mastered.

The nontraditional model, when used with young children, is based on the fact that every infant really is a "scientist in the crib" and that every child does want to make sense and is generally capable of mak-ing sense of what it is asked to do. The problem with math, as with reading, is that many who purport to use nontraditional math teaching techniques talk the talk but do not understand what they are doing, and so can not generate the results of those who use the same language but who are masters of their craft.

Constraining Assessment

Testing of students is powerful and important. It is essential in the on-going process of teaching (called formative assessment) and it is a very useful tool for gauging what has been learned (called summative assessment).

In addition, high-stakes testing can also be important because, loosely speaking, much of life consists of high-stakes tests of various kinds. Graduate students defend their theses in front of experts in the field; golfers must get through qualifying school in order to play on the professional tour; cases are argued in front of the Supreme Court and lawyers need to adjust to the court's schedule; doctors do not choose when an emergency operation is necessary—they operate when the cir-cumstances demand; the media interview public figures to suit media interests, not the interests of the public figures. All are examples of high-stakes tests to some extent.

At issue is the fact that the different models of learning and teaching that we have described have correspondingly different views of assess-ment. The guided-experience approach emphasizes performance as-sessment, some of which does have high stakes though standardized tests can be included in some situations. The exclusive tool of choice for the standard model, however, and particularly for the standardiza-tion movement, is high-stakes standardized tests.

Most teachers using aspects of the guided-experience approach peri-odically conduct short quizzes, organize assignments, pose problems and generally seek to find out what students know and what progress they are making. They also look for ways to communicate their find-ings to parents, often using a letter or number grade. Very important, however, is student self-assessment. Powerful learning relies on stu-dents grasping what they do not yet know and can not do. So students must participate in the assessment of their own development because that is the only way to make effective use of feedback. This is precisely how infants learn to talk, musicians become more adept, athletes im-prove their performance, and scientists analyze the results of their ex-periments and the methods they have used.

The argument made in support of standardized assessment are un-derstandable. In order to adequately compare how well students learn, it is said, it is necessary to test them scientifically. An objective mea-sure must be devised and implemented the same way everywhere.

The central defect in standardized testing is that it can never tell us enough about dynamic or performance knowledge. Business does not rely primarily on pencil and paper multiple choice tests in assessing competence. It uses performance assessment. Schools of music and the arts emphasize practice and rehearsal a great deal, but proficiency is largely a matter of real-world performance. Great scientists and good graduate students must know their stuff, but they reveal this knowledge primarily in the research they do and the discussions they have—not in how they respond on multiple choice tests.

No standardized test can reveal the extent to which a student has a "feel" for a subject or idea or skill. As we show in chapters 3–5, multiple modes of performance assessment in context are essential to reveal whether students have a feel for a subject or skill, what they can do as distinct from what they know, and how deep their understanding is for any specific body of ideas or skills and the degree to which they reveal creativity and a capacity for reasoning and analysis.

So the chief danger of the current push for standardized tests is that it drives a type of low-level conformity, whether educators and policymakers intend it or not. Individual student interests, talents, and expertise in specific subjects fall by the wayside. Variations in learning styles and in capacity to perform in different contexts is all too often rendered moot. Variations in child development become irrelevant. No difference is revealed in material that has been memorized for a week and material that will be the foundation of learning for a lifetime. Nothing can be seen of the difference between static knowledge (which translates more readily to tests) and dynamic knowledge (which best reveals itself in lived context). In fact, because individual differences and context do not matter when standardized testing becomes the focus of education, an essential element of powerful learning—namely the effective use of effective feedback—is driven from the system, and high-standard education is brutally short-circuited.

If the public and educators believe that standardized tests are important, they must always be seen as one element in a larger set of assessment measures that together reveal, to students themselves and to others, how well students are learning and how well schools are doing. In the preceding chapter we quote the e-mail from Mark Beach of Tahatai Coast School. The underlying thrust of his approach is to have a number of different tools that together reveal an overall pattern that acknowledge and reveal many dimensions of knowledge, skill, and capacity. Parents can see their child's work, and parents and the district can see the pattern of performance of the school as a whole.

While a cluster of measures of the sort mentioned may not allow the public to create a win-lose column in the way that sport works, and while some people who want to be "the first" or "best" may not get their egos massaged, those who care about education will gain a much better idea of how good their programs really are.

BUREAUCRATIC CHOKE HOLDS

The natural management mode of the standard model is the bureaucracy. However, the primary strengths of bureaucracies have always been to ensure conformity of practice and to resist change. That is why armies, the church, government, and large organizations have been so bureaucratic. The inevitable consequence of an *overly* bureaucratic system of public education is to preserve and sustain the standard model and make it really difficult for innovative programs or processes to succeed.

A Story

We have insisted throughout this book that deep understanding and useful knowledge require real-world experience. Sometimes to our chagrin, our own experience reconfirms the point. For instance we never fully grasped the entanglement of a school system, beliefs and ancient fears until, starting in October 1998, we participated in an attempt to create a small charter high school in a rural mountain community in Idyllwild in Southern California. We knew a great deal about learning and teaching. Our books and processes are used in many countries. However, we had never run a school. This is the story of a charter high school that opened its doors in September 1999 and had them closed a year later.

As of June 30, 1999, Idyllwild Charter High School (ICHS) had a principal, three teachers, about 40 students, an all-purpose administrative assistant, and a minuscule budget of $200,000. The teaching had been fairly good, student attendance had been superb, finances were sound, it had a viable facility (extremely difficult in a rural community with no resources), the students had performed adequately for an impoverished, start-up school on the Stanford Nine standardized test and it was in full compliance with its charter.

We should add that most of the students and parents loved the school and the community had finally begun to support it strongly, including some of the school's immediate neighbors who had rather dreaded its presence in the early days.

However, the charter was revoked, effective June 30, 1999. What happened?

The District Steps In

On the surface, two issues proved to be the school's undoing. The chartering agency, Hemet Unified School District (HUSD), found on May 2 that (although they all had at least a master's degree) the school staff were uncredentialed, in violation of law, and that they lacked finger-print clearance and so posed "a severe and imminent threat to the health or safety of the pupils" of the school. Both findings would have justified revocation. However the subsequent performance audit concluded that both findings were inappropriate. The story, in fact, is a classic example of system dysfunction.

The law required, as did the ICHS charter, that the teachers be credentialed by the Commission on Teacher Credentialing (CTC).

To follow one thread. In July 1999—two months before the school was due to open—it applied to CTC for a reciprocal credential for one teacher (we will call her Julia) already credentialed in Florida, and academically well qualified. Julia's application was returned by the state agency for unknown reasons. It was resubmitted on December 4, and this time was lost by CTC. The next application, mailed on April 20, was finally approved in July 2000, about a month after the school closed its doors.

So school began without credentialed teachers. However, it was known that hundreds of teachers in California begin each school year without credentials, so ICHS was not unduly disturbed. The delay was felt to be a normal problem that would be resolved quite soon.

In January 2000, and again by letter in February, the Hemet School District expressed concern about both credentials and finger printing. This concern, we felt, was legitimate. ICHS immediately sought the district's assistance. They referred ICHS to Riverside County offices which, after a short delay, advised the school to begin again with the CTC.

In late April, the district conducted a hearing, and at the subsequent district board meeting on May 2, the school was found to be in violation of the law, and the charter on the credentialing and finger print issues and the charter was revoked effective June 30.

The school fought to have the charter reinstated. On June 19, the day before the final motion for reinstatement, information was received from California Assemblyman Jim Batin's office. His staff advised ICHS that under the California Education Code, the County had power to issue teachers with temporary certificates on proof of submission to CTC of a valid credential application—something the ICHS lawyer did not know! That is, because it was known that credentials might take some time to acquire, there was a way for the county to make it legally possible for all new teachers to begin teaching immediately! Moreover, not only was this known by the County, it was standard procedure. That is how the large number of uncredentialed teachers in California—and Riverside County—and Hemet Unified School District—can begin teaching without violating the law.

This information was faxed to the District Superintendent and the Board but was discounted at the final hearing.

The tale of fingerprinting is similarly twisted because it transpired that the school had to register as a district and receive a code of its own in order to conduct fingerprinting independently of HUSD. However, it also became evident that had there been any real belief that the students were in imminent danger, the District could have administered fingerprinting to all the school's staff at any time and have the results back within a few days.

The performance audit (Jacobs, 2000) conducted by a volunteer high-profile management consultant and former educator, read, in part, as follows:

> They were successful educationally, had developed the administrative experience required and had the wholehearted support of the parents and community. The operation was a success, but the patient died. (p. 2)

And further, "Perhaps the primary problem was a clash of cultures, but there was no need to terminate the school" (p. 43).

We were, and still are, upset, and understand the aphorism that "experience is what you get when you don't get what you want." We now know the effort it takes to establish a new school. We understand better than we ever did before, the legitimate initial caution in a community about a school that looks different, and the way in which support can be developed over time. We admire the willingness of so many parents and others to take a risk and support a new endeavor, sometimes through their effort and sometimes through gifts and loans. We appreciate more than ever the demands on those working within a school, both to do their prescribed job (teach and administer) and to attend to their additional real work (substitute for many parents, provide health care, work with social services, and so on). We have better grasped the fact that even idealists have to work in a real world and deal with the law and the larger system as they are (and not as they should be).

Some Lessons

At the same time as our eyes were opened to the practical needs of running a school, we also gained a much better appreciation of the underlying dynamics that keep things as they are, and of the issues that need to be dealt with if substantial improvement of education is ever to occur. We have a really good feel for the system. Even with the best will in the world, bureaucracies tend to absorb and dilute change so that the new ends up looking very much like the old.

1. *System issues are real.* Irrespective of how innovative a program is, a host of everyday issues needs to be dealt with satisfactorily. Almost every aspect of system requirements, from personnel to finance, must be addressed, even by those running very innovative programs. Sustaining an idealistic spirit and adopting innovative practices whilst seeking to comply with system requirements is extremely difficult. For example, the time line for our charter school was driven by the availability of one volunteer who put in most of the preliminary work, and by a small window of access to the only possible facility in our rural village. The consequence is that we began too soon and lacked hardnosed but nurturing leadership. We paid the price for being more idealistic than practical. A measure of both is indispensable.

2. *The set-up:* The standard model organizes students by age, grade, and subject. Individual courses need to be taught in specific classes with a specified number of instructional minutes to be offered each semester. Experience-based education thrives on projects where several different subjects may be integrated. For example, most complex science projects can not be packaged into a single 45-minute class, or even into a series of such classes over several weeks. Authentic experiments take large, ongoing blocks of time. Yet, in the ICHS charter, for instance, the district insisted that subjects be defined and minutes counted in traditional ways. This forced our three teachers to conduct many more individual classes than we had originally contemplated, and made it impossible to capitalize on the very good staff/student ration of about 1 to 15. Thus, in complying with many of the initial district requirements, we were set up from the beginning to function like a traditional school. Sometimes a compromise is possible. However, if a system narrowly construes, and then rigidly mandates, each state requirement, the rigid structure that is established will make it almost impossible for innovations to be implemented.

3. *A culture of compliance:* Districts are dominated by issues of compliance with the law and fears of legal liability. Hemet, for instance, has been successfully sued on several occasions. Charter schools are in-

tended to be free of many system constraints and yet are supervised by the system from which they are meant to be freed. The fox is well and truly in charge of the hen house. This is a difficult, and often impossible, tension. It is absurd to believe that those chartering agencies immersed in a bureaucratic and fearful mind-set will necessarily have the willingness or the capacity to work with new schools that require the taking of some risks and the giving of some leeway (as intended by charter law) and opportunity to learn how things work. For similar reasons, innovative programs and teachers in the regular system are at the mercy of those who do not understand or support them.

4. *Rules and regulations designed to ensure compliance with the system consume a disproportionate amount of resources.* The amount of bureaucratic entanglement that the school experienced was substantial. The amount faced by every noncharter public school is almost incomprehensible. They must deal with building codes, employee relationships and personnel requirements, matters of health and safety, credentialing requirements, volumes of paperwork associated with every grant that they might receive, curriculum requirements and standards, and much, much more. The requirements drain energy, consume resources, frequently blindside administrators, and make it extremely difficult to adequately focus on students and teaching.

5. *Vested interests:* The Hemet Board had the power to reinstate the school, and evidence of public support and compliance on all issues justified reinstatement. It still refused to act. We discovered that when issues become personal (as they did with ICHS) the people with power in the system tend to prevail. It should be added that the larger system is rife with vested interests competing for power that have the effect of stifling innovation. For example:

- Teachers' unions tend to support notions such as pay for instructional minutes, for instance. This view of learning as defined in terms of time spent in front of students radically inhibits dynamic experiential teaching and learning. In dynamic environments, it is extremely difficult to find ways to count minutes in a subject specific way, and the attainment of high standards are not driven by "seat time."
- People often compete for election to the school board because membership serves ideological, business, or personal needs. In those circumstances, many board votes serve personal goals and satisfy personal agendas, and the interests of good education are discounted.
- Many businesses thrive in the present system. For example, a curriculum organized in traditional ways is a haven for the multibil-

lion dollar textbook and testing industry because it makes the design of books simple and the marketing easy. Hence much of the standardization movement is fed by corporations with a vested interest in "business as usual," and many schools and districts with views of their own are forced by state decisions to pay for materials sold to the state by business.

6. *Funding and resources:* Adequate funding is crucial. The ICHS began with nothing, though after it was launched it did receive a start-up grant from the state, one of very few awarded. But it had no money for facilities and no guarantee of how many students would attend when it opened its doors. It was saved in the early months, when relations were still fairly good, by a loan from the district to be repaid from state funding. The very difficult problem the system faces is how to choose what to fund and how to hold recipients accountable for spending money appropriately. The natural tendency is to provide funding with strings attached. The practical consequence is that funding basically serve interests and practices supported by the system. Thus, the values and procedures of the system perpetuate themselves. That is one reason why there is a growing push for vouchers that enable parents and clusters of citizens to decide for themselves how their children should be educated.

THE STANDARDIZATION MOVEMENT
PRODUCES A CLIMATE OF FEAR AND STRESS

All the above problems are reinforced by stress, fear, and helplessness. The greatest weakness of the standardization movement is that, in the name of rewards, punishments, and accountability, it drives educators into a mode where good teaching vanishes and survival prevails. This message is understandably difficult for the public to grasp. For instance, business has used incentive-based management for decades. However, many of the traditional practices of business and management have been heavily criticized for many years by leading practitioners and organizational consultants. Thus, the father of total quality management, W. Edwards Deming (2000) insisted that organizations should do everything possible to drive out fear. The standardization movement is flying in the face of the most important findings and practices of the last two decades.

In chapter 2 we described the survival response of fight or flight and introduced the notion of downshifting. The unfortunate corollary of much of turmoil in education is that many people, including the best and the brightest of the teachers and administrators, are downshifted. Many parents and school board members are in the same boat. One result is that much of the initiative, creativity, risk taking, and high performance that we seek is being leeched out of the system. Another is that very, very harmful practices are being introduced into classrooms and schools for the specific purpose of spiking test scores. We have had countless discussions about this problem throughout the United States and elsewhere. Research is now beginning to confirm what we have observed (McNeil & Valenzuela, 2000).

It works like this. The culture, through the use of standards, high-stakes tests, accountability, and mega-bureaucracies, is setting objectives that must be met. Failure results in loss of income, loss of face, and, sometimes, loss of a job. This is an issue of survival. The next point is that methods of teaching are being heavily prescribed. For experts in their craft many of these mandated methods are nonsense. So in order to survive they are required to give up doing what they do well and actually aim for lower results assessed in more limited ways then they currently use themselves. Sometimes the only indicator used is performance of students in a specific grade, irrespective of any other factors—including the performance of those same students in prior years, let alone their performance using other types of assessment. At the same time, with more and more media interest, the actions and results of educators are fully exposed. Now the survival issue is accompanied by helplessness. And so adults downshift.

One solution is to leave the system. That has actually happened for decades. Between 20 percent and 50 percent of new teachers quit within five years of being on the job, and teacher retention is a major problem for public education. A very large number of those lost to the profession are the very ones who can function effectively in dynamic environments, and resist contexts that are highly standardized. Those teachers can be found succeeding in every walk of life in the outside world.

A second solution is to batten down the hatches, ride out the storm, hide in a cave, and basically protect themselves in any way that they can. In this state of mind, some very clear psychological responses take place.

- Downshifted people become less aware of what is going on around them and do not see cues that could help them. This is called "narrowing of the perceptual field" (Combs, 1988). They revert back to the use of methods based upon their own prior experience! Thus, many schools in states such as California and Texas now have students spending several hours every week practicing for the standardized tests instead of working to learn something new and more demanding.

- Downshifted people are much less willing to take risks, seeking instead to please and placate those with the power to reward and punish (Deci & Ryan, 1987; Kohn, 1993). That is why many teachers are taking steps to ensure that their students prepare specifically for tests to be taken in the near future, rather than deal with wider issues, more complex ideas, or groundwork for future years (McNeil & Valenzuela, 2000).

- Downshifted people literally lose access to some of their own higher order functioning (Caine & Caine, 1994; LeDoux, 1996) and so become less adept at solving problems and making the system work. In this mental and emotional state, even though there is plenty of evidence that the guided-experience approach can work in most states right now, and that students will do better on standardized tests anyway, there is even more reluctance than previously to do the work needed to take education into the 21st century and support more powerful approaches.

- Downshifted people become more adversarial and territorial, less able to rise above their feelings and opinions, and less capable of working together with those who have different goals and beliefs (Hart, 1983; McLean, 1978).

This pattern is well understood and perfectly obvious in everyday life. Here, for instance, is a comment by Tubby Smith, assistant coach to the U.S. Olympic basketball team that won the gold medal at the Sydney games but did not function as a team as well as expected: "What happens is in a tight situation, when they get stressed and the game's close, they revert back to what they know best" (*Los Angeles Times,* 10/3/2000, D8).

In short, many aspects of the high standards—standardization movements accomplish precisely the opposite of what is intended. While some bad teachers may have to leave the system, some bad schools close down, and many inadequate teachers have to acquire greater skills (all of which we support), many of the people who can perform at higher levels—or who are learning to do so—are forced to adapt to the basics. It is not high standards that are being achieved. While some really low standards in some limited subgroups are being raised, in general, it is mediocrity and worse that is being standardized.

THE HIDDEN CURRICULUM

All systems are grounded in a set of compelling core beliefs and underlying assumptions, and those competing beliefs have enormous power. Dawkins, a British biologist, coined the term "meme" to describe a cultural belief that literally has a life of its own. A meme starts as an idea but ultimately has the power to organize and structure society in a specific way.

> Although we might initially adopt memes because they are useful, it is often the case that after a certain point they begin to affect our actions and thoughts in ways that are at best ambiguous and at worst definitely not in our interest. (Csikszentmihalyi, 1993, p.123)

We suggest that the standard model is, in fact, an expression of some memes—ideas that are so powerful that they have taken on a life of their own, irrespective of evidence that reveals their inadequacy.

The hidden curriculum of the standard model is a belief system. Bureaucracies are social systems that think they are machines. In every aspect of the way that standard education is organized, the subtle message is that people and systems function like machines, that success depends on control and management of all the details, that results can be predicted and timed, that methods for getting there can be cast in stone, and that educators and students can not really be trusted to keep on task or do what needs to be done without the use of power, rewards, and punishment. But in the words of the popular song, "it ain't necessarily so."

The challenge is not to let go of control but to share control, as illustrated in the examples discussed in chapter 6. The standard model is what Eisler calls a "dominator hierarchy" (1987). It is controlled from the top. It simply can not provide the opportunities for powerful learning and great teaching that the times demand. Education needs to open itself up to the best of what is now known about learning organizations. While roles and functions must still be specified to some extent, standards that are an order of magnitude above what currently occurs depends on a sharing of power with high expectations and accountability being demanded of everyone. The essence of the problem of radically improving education is, ultimately, to change the beliefs of enough people about how high-powered learning and great teaching work. And then to create the conditions where they can flourish.

BRAKE

MARSHALL

CHAPTER 8

The Competitive Edge

Given the right circumstances, from no more than dreams, deter-
mination, and the liberty to try, quite ordinary people consistently
do extraordinary things. (Hock, 1999, p. 192)

It is time to revisit the crisis in education that we introduced in the first
chapter. The system of public education is very deeply entrenched in
law and culture, in part because it is so deeply aligned with other parallel beliefs and practices. However, the pressures for change are also
immense, and so there is a more profound and deeper crisis than has
been appreciated.

THE EDGE OF POSSIBILITY

As we have seen, turbulence is being generated in several ways:

- There is profound dissatisfaction with the way that the system is
  functioning, both academically and from the point of view of the
  safety of children.
- A desire for more parental choice and control over the education
  of their children is moving from the sidelines to midfield.
- The lure of the profits to be made from education and the desire on
  the part of business to influence the "product" that schools put out
  is great, and the influence of business is substantial.
- The speed and extent of networking facilitated by the World Wide
  Web is bringing resources to people who did not have them, creating
  partnerships where none were possible, and generally building networks that are permeating and surrounding the traditional system.

- More and more is becoming known about how the brain/mind learns, and it is slowly becoming incontrovertible that lived experience can dramatically enhance teaching and learning when done well.
- In many sectors there is a hunger for community and a longing to belong that could be, but is not being, met by the traditional education system.
- There is a visceral tension between the standardization high-standards movement and the experience-driven high-standards movement.
- Politicians of every stripe are willing to capitalize on every thread in this complex tangle of beliefs and practices.
- The media randomly but intensely shines a light on every aspect of the many dilemmas.
- The tension is heightened because the whole situation is rife with paradox.
- While many in the world of business call for schooling that produces people with initiative, creativity, and a global view, many in the business world (including some calling for these new kinds of students) also benefit enormously from the profits to be earned from the standard model, a model that prevents the desired qualities from being developed in students.
- Technobusiness tends to be extremely materialistic, while many homeschoolers and educators have very different values. And yet the facilities offered by Technobusiness provide a superb platform by means of which those with different values can work together.
- Much of the advice being offered by business for the management of schools is based on a standard model of business, and that model is being seriously questioned by leaders in the field of organizational development. Thus, Dee Hock (1999) the founder of the VISA, and Meg Wheatley (1999) author of one of the most influential books written about organizations, both contend that the normal way of running and managing organizations no longer works.
- Many of the people most disaffected by public education are ardent advocates of public education. Yet they are turning to charters, vouchers, and homeschool in attempts to see their visions implemented.

- Homeschooling parents are demanding the freedom to educate their own children, yet they are often at odds with each other. Some want freedom to provide children with an opportunity to make their own choices, while others want freedom to make sure that their children do not choose alternative values or views.
- Although an unprecedented amount of time, money, and effort is being devoted to reforming education, most of those advocating change (both educators and noneducators) are ignorant about how children learn.

Meanwhile, the current tensions, supplemented by the possibilities created by the World Wide Web, are exponentially increasing the educational networking between people and organizations. Here are just some of the developing relationships. In some of these we will find people and groups, once thought to be at loggerheads or at least unconnected with each other, coming together in totally unexpected ways. They include:

- Projects being undertaken by people of different ages in different contexts working together on different sides of the nation—or the planet;
- Charter schools flourishing in many regions, and beginning to expand across district and state borders;
- Homeschoolers pooling resources, using technology, and engaging in collective homeschooling.
- Homeschool networks entering into marriages of convenience with traditional schools, e.g. by combining with programs of independent study or by leasing local school facilities at nights and on weekends;
- Providers of distance education entering into partnerships with local government schools;
- Entire virtual schools being created;
- Superb, self-employed, itinerant teachers contracting out to work with local communities, homeschoolers, and virtual schools;
- States setting up districts of homeschoolers, networking with each other.

- Government systems pooling resources, and opening themselves to mass distance education.
- Megacorporations setting up their own virtual and local learning environments, partnering with government and homeschool entities;
- Partnerships of corporations, homeschoolers, and private schools and organizations when they all have a common core interest such as a spiritual path.

The crisis is painful, but it may also be necessary. All the turmoil shows that many of the foundations and fundamental assumptions of public education are now being questioned. Together, the dissatisfaction and turbulence reveal a system that is very unstable and is approaching what is often called the "edge of chaos." We prefer to call it the edge of possibility (Caine & Caine, 1997).

TAKING ACTION

While the standard model of schooling can be improved, and we support some efforts to improve it, that model is inherently incapable of providing the high-standard education that is needed for survival and success in the twenty-first century and beyond. Education *must* help students acquire more performance knowledge and place much less emphasis on surface knowledge. For that reason the indispensable core of the change that needs to be made is to implement the guided-experience approach. Our collective task is to bring clarity to the goal, nurture efforts already underway, and to create the conditions within which a guided-experience approach can thrive.

While none of us can control the direction that education takes, acting together we can influence that direction significantly. The point to emphasize is that education is ultimately driven by the beliefs and mental models that people have. Hence, the indispensable key step in influencing the future is to influence core beliefs of enough of those who have an impact on education, and to act in accordance with those new beliefs.

In terms of how social systems work, the process that takes place is called self-reference (Wheatley, 1999). That means that each of the individual participants acts in accordance with what he or she wants and thinks is most important, and each interprets whatever happens in the light of what he or she believes. The system that springs up is the outcome of all these different individual interpretations and actions. It reflects the values and beliefs of the people within them. However,

> *It is easy to talk service and think profit.*
> *It is easy to talk spirit and think power.*
> *It is easy to preach community and think self.*

It is not what people say that matters, but what they actually value and believe in the core of their being. The key is for enough of us to take the new principles of learning seriously, and to act accordingly. Here, we suggest, are critical actions that need to be taken on a wide scale.

Expose Unstated Assumptions about Learning and Teaching

In most proposals for changing education that have received great exposure in recent times, and this includes almost every action taken by every level of government, negligible attention has been paid to how people actually learn. There is an extraordinary degree of taken-for-granted ignorance.

We need to allow the light of day to shine on these unexamined beliefs. And the way to do that is to ask questions of anyone who seeks to "change" or "reform" education. How, precisely, do they think people learn? What factors contribute to meaningful learning? What is the difference between knowing something and knowing about something? How does one take into consideration the fact that all people, infants included, develop at different rates? To what extent did they learn from experience and/or direct instruction? What evidence do they have to support their views about learning? What have they read about recent research into the nature of learning and brain functioning?

It does not matter whether the person asking the question knows the answer. What matters is that the issue be drawn into the open. And this can be done by anyone, anywhere. During family meals, at work, through letters to the editor, in clubs, on line, at parent and teacher meetings, during political campaigns, waiting to see the doctor, town hall meetings, and so on. Listen to the answers, think about them, and if you feel it is appropriate, just ask another question.

A red flag to notice, and pounce on, is anyone who offers a simpleminded sound bite as a solution to or explanation for the whole problem.

"Standards and accountability" may camouflage the lowering of standards and escape from real accountability.

"Oppose vouchers because they take money from public education" simply does not deal with the extent to which money is wasted on public education.

"Parents know best" is true for some parents, but what about those who allow their children to watch four hours of junk television a night or gorge on junk food?

It is easy, and popular, to use the language of powerful education to mask simplistic and trite education. And many of those in government, business, and education readily and easily use such language. The first essential task in changing the meme is to expose the assumptions that underlie what people propose, and to not be detoured by what people say.

The problem is compounded for two reasons:

First, researchers, practitioners, and the media use the same term to mean different things. Examples are "brain-based learning," "whole language" and "high standards."

Second, research can be used and abused. One practice is to use the phrase "according to the research" when no real research is provided or when facts and evidence are misrepresented, as has happened in the reading wars. Another is to challenge the integrity of researchers rather than examine what they say.

The best solution that we have found is to ask questions, and to keep asking questions. We also use the filter of the principles and practices spelled out in this book to guide us in the questions we ask. Hopefully they can be of value to you as well.

Support Leading-Edge Programs and People

One of the most damaging consequences of the standardization movement has been the elimination of really powerful programs and the loss to the system of really great teachers. It is essential for the public to support people and programs who manifestly implement the principles and practices of the guided-experience approach to education. This book can be used to provide indicators of what to look for. There is no limit to the number of ways in which these practices take place, but the essence should always be there. For instance:

Standards: Teachers should really know their subject and be able to articulate the standards, essential skills, and knowledge they are embedding in whatever is happening. Even in a noisy and active classroom the teacher should be able to articulate what is happening and explain why.

Community and motivation: There should be evidence of mutual respect between teachers and students. Both students and teachers should be willing and free to ask hard questions. There should be evidence that students want classes and projects to continue beyond the prescribed times.

Instruction: There should be "global experiences"of various sorts. Students should be regularly engaged in research. Teachers should be asking challenging questions, guiding thinking, providing feedback, and pushing for quality.

Assessment: There should be ongoing assessment. Students should participate in assessing their own progress and identifying areas in which they need to improve. There should be opportunities for students to produce and perform in multiple settings. If standardized tests are used, they should *not* be the primary focus of attention of students or teacher, and they should be taken in stride.

We appreciate the difficulty, sometimes, of sifting the wheat from the chaff. In this event we suggest that you identify some teacher whose students score well on orthodox tests as well as clearly being able to perform well in the arena of life. The odds are that such a teacher knows what she is talking about, and can be a good initial contact and guide as you decide what action to take.

Campaign for the Release of Brakes on High-Powered Learning

No system can flourish if a lid is placed on what can be accomplished. Imagine, for instance, striving to produce great athletes by eliminating world class events, or encouraging the development of great scientists by closing down the best graduate schools. While upgrading public education generally is an immensely difficult endeavor, two initial steps are clear. The larger system needs to release the brakes on those elements of the system that have the opportunity to flourish and produce exceptional results. And those seeking to take advantage of the opportunities offered need to have a sufficient alignment of the elements that lead to excellent teaching and powerful learning.

Charter schools: Charter schools are being introduced into public education in the United States to provide a voice for alternative ways to educate children. We know that they vary enormously, and that by our criteria some are capable and some are incapable of doing a very good job. Nevertheless, the express purpose is to reduce the choke holds of bureaucracy so that good education can flourish. For success to occur, we agree with Finn et al. (2000) that there are some essential core features of good charter law. For example:

There should be multiple chartering agencies so that innovative schools are not obliged to satisfy the requirements of hostile supervisory districts or charter agencies.

There must be an appeals process both for initial petitions that are denied and for charters that are revoked.

There must be funding for plant and infrastructure, and not only for basic salaries.

Nothing is better able to prevent success than the absence of basic resources.

With these and other measures in place, charter schools can flourish and, as a minimum, provide examples and inspiration for others. Indeed, there are successes, such as the Minnesota New Country School House and others that perform precisely this leadership role.

Information age curriculum: The standardization movement correctly sees an explosion in the amount of information coursing through the culture. The solution that is adopted, in the name of raising standards, is for the curriculum to cover more ground. That is simply the wrong solution. There is no conceivable way in which more than a small fraction of the available information will ever be absorbed by any human being. Adequate coverage is impossible.

The way to handle large amounts of information is for people to think in terms of more complex ideas because information is ultimately organized on the basis of ideas. That means that the central thrust of curriculum development and the setting of standards in the United States and many other countries has to change direction. The goal needs to be for students to naturally think in terms of ideas and categories that have wide-scale application. Although we can not go into the issue here, ultimately the very beliefs that underlie curriculum (such as the belief that the world works like a machine) will have to be called into question. For the time being, look for and support any approach to curriculum that is organized around ideas that make it possible to see powerful and meaningful relations and connections between different subjects.

Decouple standardized methods and standardized tests, and support authentic assessment: If standardized tests are so deeply embedded in the public psyche that they are with us for the foreseeable future, it is imperative to at least free teachers to achieve prescribed results by using their own professional skill and discretion. The alternative is roughly like asking doctors to save lives by reading the directions of surgical text books as they operate. To this freedom must be added information about those aspects of the curriculum that tests are going to cover. We are not suggesting test questions be supplied, only that curriculum and testing be aligned. The thought that they could ever be unaligned is incomprehensible to us, but that lack of alignment has, nevertheless, been standard practice for years in many education systems.

Next, it is essential to introduce modes of assessment based on relatively authentic performance, and for those modes to matter when results are decided. By way of example, the Bill and Melinda Gates Foundation makes significant grants to high-performing schools, districts, and networks. One of the criteria they use to identify successful schools is performance assessment:

> *Performance Assessment:* Clear expectations define what students should know and be able to do; students produce quality work products and present to real audiences; student work shows evidence of understanding, not just recall; assessment tasks allow students to exhibit higher-order thinking; and teachers and students set learning goals and monitor progress. (www.gatesfoundation.org)

They add in another section that

> *Data-driven decisions shape a dynamic structure and schedule.* In other words, the administration and management of the school should adjust so that the teaching that leads to high performance learning, and the demonstration of high performance learning, are both possible.

Campaign for Twenty-First Century Teacher Training and Professional Development

The standard model is alive and well in the minds of many teacher educators and in many (and perhaps most) programs of professional development at school, district, state, and college levels. The model and the approach to training and development of educators must change.

We outline our approach to professional development in the final chapter of our book, "Unleashing the Power of Perceptual Change" (*Education on the Edge of Possibility,* 1997).

1. Educators must have an up-to-date grasp of how people learn. We use our 12 principles of learning as our frame of reference.
2. Educators must be proficient in the guided-experience approach to teaching.
3. Educators must be at home with the power and networking capacities of technology.
4. Educators must be expert in a chosen field and must see relationship embedded between every field.
5. Educators must master the personal qualities inherent in the art of building relationship and forming learning communities with each other, students, and the broader public, and must see coercive discipline as secondary and as a fallback.
6. Professional development must practice what it preaches. Those who cannot work with the guided-experience approach have no business being teachers of teachers.

Seek and Support Natural Partners

The standard model and the standardization movement are not just ways of schooling. They reflect a deeply held view about how the world itself works—called a paradigm—and they are an expression of a cluster of social systems and beliefs that are aligned with each other. For example, a heavy-handed approach to school is often accompanied by a heavy-handed approach to law and order. And the standard model is a natural feeding ground for many businesses.

The guided-experience approach, and the additional possibilities inherent in it, need also to be aligned with natural partners. We need to find ways to work with others who share similar views about what it means to be human and how reality itself works. Even within the world of public education, groups with strongly aligned philosophies and practices tend to ignore each other, yet could pool resources and act together. For instance, there is an immense overlap of ideas and expertise in the practice of experiential education (outdoors education), good arts education, and good reading programs.

The daunting challenge for us in the larger society is that many of the opposites that have been taken for granted for decades, sometimes centuries, need to be rethought. Traditionally state run schools and homeschooling have been opposed to each other. But we know that some educators and some parents have identical views about great education. In the United States, and some other countries, church and state have been kept at arms length, and many educators view the intrusion of religion into public education with horror. And yet there are some approaches to the spiritual life, including the authentic pursuit of deep meaning, that provides students with an energy for meaningful learning sadly lacking in most public education. Some businesses profit by draining the life out of schools, yet there are many in the business world who share and practice the beliefs and principles spelled out in this book.

The time has come to find a way to transcend differences without violating ourselves. That is the thrust of a grand experiment that is being carried out throughout the world. The task involves more than joint projects, discussions, debate, or consensus. It involves a way of communicating that respects the individual while simultaneously generating a much more powerful collective. One approach was initiated by physicist David Bohm (Bohm, 1987), the founding father of a movement called "dialogue." Dialogue has, as its goal, the promotion of the flow of meaning between people so that even those (such as owners and unionists) who have traditionally been at loggerheads with each other can begin to see where their deeper community lies.

> The intention of dialogue is to reach new understanding and, in doing so, to form a totally new basis from which to think and act. In dialogue, one not only solves problems, one dissolves them. (Isaacs, 1999, p. 19)

Our own endeavor is by means of four-day institutes, originally developed with two colleagues, which we run under the name "Gossamer Ridge" (www.Gossamerridge.com). Our purpose is to bring leaders in various fields together in optimal learning environments in order to explore such issues as "Enhancing learning by making the invisibles visible". One goal is to create a stimulating yet contemplative state of mind in people racing to keep up in an unnaturally fast world. We do so in part by integrating the arts (which are a powerful means of engaging a whole person and building community) into high-level discussion. In that context we collectively explore leading edge ideas and practices about learning and systems.

The challenge is coming to grips with a way of thinking and acting that blends chaos and order, competition and cooperation. When they function together, the vast reserves and properties of systems are released and activated. The essential thread is that power, and powerful learning, resides in the pooling of resources and the sharing of possibilities. What matters is how we learn together.

THRIVING ON THE EDGE

We wrote in chapter 2 that "in the thirty thousand years prior to the Renaissance and the Industrial Revolution—for hunter gatherers, farmers, crafts people, and others—the way of learning and teaching was simple. All groups used some type of apprenticeship."

Apprenticeship has now come full circle. Many in the public are calling for students who are creative, mature, and knowledgeable enough to function well in a rapidly changing world. Yet the predominant approach to educational reform at this point in time is to standardize and control The context within which children are learning is fundamentally incompatible with what they need to learn. A rigid, hierarchical context prepares people for a rigid, unchanging life—one found in prisons, factories, and the like. The standard model, and standardization, sabotage, undermine and constrain the essential learnings needed for success in the twenty-first century.

The larger message is that the culture itself must live the conditions that it needs to engender in education. Change simply cannot be forced from above nor imposed on educators or the public. Nor is it a matter of summit meetings that lead to consensus on the basis of which change is imposed. Learning and education can not be seen as limited aspects of the larger system. Rather, every aspect of life educates, and learning is an ongoing act of life. Really high-powered education thrives in an authentically democratic system—one in which participants are respected and honored so that their mental, emotional, and spiritual capacities can be accessed and can contribute to the whole.

However, such a system is *not* a laissez-faire enterprise in which anything goes. If we want students to be rigorous in their thinking, then we must be rigorous in our thinking; if we want students to be courteous and respectful of others, then we must be courteous and respectful of others; if we insist that students learn and that educators be open to and accept feedback, then we have to learn and be open to and openly accept feedback.

Ultimately, the key to high standards is the extent to which we are willing to put ourselves on the line.

The education systems that will best equip children for the future will be those where the system itself models and lives the essence of what it is that children need to learn. Good science is taught in environments conducive to good science being done; critical thinking only becomes real, personal, and dynamic in environments where it is encouraged and used in the course of everyday life. Creativity and initiative are fostered in environments that support risk taking. Such environments encourage learning from mistakes, reflective analysis of what actually happens, and the opportunity to go back and do it again without being punished.

Everything that is now known about powerful learning points to the need to align the best of learning and teaching with the best of the larger culture. As the principles and practices of complex adaptive systems take hold (Wheatley, 1999)—in the economy, the World Wide Web, and elsewhere—those same principles and practices need to inform education and schooling. And of all the factors that drive the learning of children, nothing is more important to them than to be immersed in a world in which most of the adults take learning seriously. We don't mean just the accumulation of facts and skills. We mean the sort of learning that places beliefs and assumptions on center stage as warranting continual testing and exploration. When children are immersed in these environments, the power of the apprentice community and the learning brain are linked.

There will be a price to pay. The time has come to allow our children to know more and to become more intelligent than we are. This is not an invitation for precocious adolescents to play at being discourteous smart alecs. Rather it is to say that a new way of being brings with it new possibilities, and younger brains and minds are better equipped to appreciate and grasp those possibilities than are most adults. Giving— genuinely giving—our children these opportunities and supporting them in their explorations will not be easy. But for any group of people, and any culture, that keeps the long term in mind, activating and nurturing the brain power of its children is an indispensable key to sustaining a competitive edge.

Bibliography

Abbott, J. & Ryan T. (2000). *The unfinished revolution.* Alexandria, VA.: Association for Supervision and Curriculum Development.

Allington, R. L. & Woodside-Jiron, H. (1999, November). The politics of literacy teaching: How "research" shaped education policy. *Educational Researcher, 28*(8), 4–13.

Allport, S. (1986). *Explorers of the black box: The search for the cellular basis of memory.* New York: W. W. Norton.

Archer, J. (2000, January). Under Amato, Hartford schools show progress. *Education Week, XIX*(25), 1, 18–19.

Ashby, F. G., Isen, A. M., & Turken, U. (1999, July). A neuropsychological theory of positive affect and its influence on cognition. *Psychological Review, 106*(3), 529–50.

Bandura, A. (1992). Self-efficacy mechanism in sociocognitive functioning. Annual meeting of the American Educational Research Association.

Bennett, W. J., Finn, C. H., Jr., & Cribb, J. T. E., Jr. (1999). *The educated child.* New York: Free Press.

Bohm, D. (1987). *Unfolding meaning: A weekend of dialogue with David Bohm.* New York: ARK Paperbacks.

Bransford, J. D., Brown, A. L., & Cocking, R. R. (eds.) (1999). *How people learn: Brain, mind, experience, and school.* National Research Council. Washington, DC: National Academy Press.

Brothers, L. (1997). *Friday's footprint: How society shapes the human mind.* New York: Oxford University Press.

Bruner, J., Goodnow, J., & Austin, G. A. (1967). *A study of thinking.* New York: Wiley.

Caine, R. (2000, November). Building a bridge from research to the classroom. *Educational Leadership, 58*(3), 59–61. See unabridged version at www.Cainelearning.com.

Caine, R., & Caine, G. (1994). *Making connections: Teaching and the human brain.* Menlo Park, CA: Addison Wesley Longman.

Caine, R., & Caine, G. (1997). *Education on the edge of possibility.* Alexandria, VA: Association for Supervision and Curriculum Development.

Caine, G., Caine, R., & Crowell, S. (1999). *Mindshifts* (2nd ed.). Tucson, AZ: Zephyr Press.

Capra, F. (1997). *The web of life: A new understanding of living systems.* New York: Doubleday.

Capra, F. (2000). *Ecoliteracy: Mapping the terrain.* Berkeley, CA: The Center for Ecoliteracy.

Claxton, G. (1997). *Hare brain, tortoise mind: How intelligence increases when you think less.* New York: ECCO Press.

A Coalition for Self-Learning. (2000). *Creating learning communities.* www. creatinglearningcommunities.org.

Cole, K. C. (1999, October 13). Nobel prizes go to Caltech chemist, Dutch physicists. *Los Angeles Times,* pp. 1, 15.

Coles, G. (2000). *Misreading reading: The bad science that hurts children.* Portsmouth, NH: Heinenmann.

Colfax, D. & Colfax, M. (1988). *Home schooling for excellence: How to take charge of your child's education and why you absolutely must.* New York: Warner Books.

Combs, A., Richards, A. C., & Richards, F. (1988). *Perceptual psychology: A humanistic approach to the study of persons.* Lanham, MD: University Press of America.

Coulson, A. J. (1999). *Market education: The unknown history.* New Brunswick, NJ: Transaction Publishers.

Covey, S. R. (1989). *The seven habits of highly effective people: Powerful lessons in personal change.* New York: Simon & Schuster.

Csikszentmihalyi, M. (1990). *Flow: The psychology of optimal experience.* New York: Harper Perennial.

Csikszentmihalyi, M. (1993). *The evolving self: A psychology for the third millennium.* New York: HarperCollins.

Damasio, A. R. (1994). *Descartes' error: Emotion, reason and the human brain.* New York: Avon Books.

Damasio, A. R. (1999). *The feeling of what happens: Body and emotion in the making of consciousness.* New York: Harcourt Brace.

Deci, E. L., & Ryan, R. M. (1987). The support of autonomy and the control of behavior. *Journal of Personality and Social Psychology, 53*(6), 1024–1037.

Deming, W. E. (2000). *Out of the crisis*. Cambridge, MA: MIT Press.

Diamond, M. (1988). *Enriching heredity: The impact of the environment on the anatomy of the brain*. New York: Free Press.

Dickinson, E. (1924). *The complete poems*. Boston: Little Brown.

Dryden, G., & Vos, J. (1993). *The learning revolution*. Rolling Hills Estates, CA: Jalmar Press.

Duncan, S. (1998). *Making TV watching selective*. Montana State University Communication Services.

Eisler, R. (1987). *The chalice and the blade*. San Francisco: Harper & Row.

Edwards, C., Gandini, L., & Forman, G. (1996). *The hundred languages of children: The Reggio Emilia approach to early childhood education*. Norwood, NJ: Ablex Publishing Corporation.

Fadiman, D. (1988). *Why do these kids love school?* (Video tape). Menlo Park, CA: Concentric Media.

Festinger, L. (1957). *A theory of cognitive dissonance*. Stanford, CA: Stanford University Press.

Finn, C. E., Jr., Manno, B. V., & Vanourek G. (2000). *Charter schools in action: Renewing public education*. Princeton, NJ: Princeton University Press.

Gendlin, E. T. (1981). *Focusing* (2nd ed.). New York: Bantam.

Goldberg, S. (2001). *The executive brain: Frontal lobes and the civilized mind*. New York: Oxford University Press.

Goleman, D. (1995). *Emotional intelligence: Why it can matter more than IQ*. New York: Bantam.

Gopnik, A., Meltsoff, A. N., & Kuhl, P. (1999). *The scientist in the crib: Minds, brains, and how children learn*. New York: William Morrow.

Halpern, D. (1989). *Thought and knowledge: An introduction to critical thinking*. Hillsdale, NJ: Lawrence Erlbaum.

Haney, W. (2000, August 19). The myth of the Texas miracle in education. In Gene V. Glass (ed.), *Education Policy Analysis Archives*, 8(41). A peer-reviewed scholarly electronic journal. College of Education. Arizona State University.

Harrison, E., & King, S. (1999, September 24). George C. Scott dies at 71; refused Oscar for *Patton*. *Los Angeles Times*, pp. A1, A25.

Hart, L. (1983). *Human brain & human learning*. New York: Longman.

Hillman, J. (1996). *The soul's code: In search of character and calling*. New York: Warner Books.

Hirshberg, C. (1999, September). How good are our schools? *Life*, 40, 43.

Hock, D. (1999). *Birth of the Chaordic Age*. San Franciso Berrett-Koehler.

Holmes, O. W. (1881). *The common law*. Boston: Little, Brown.

Isaacs, W. (1999). *Dialogue and the art of thinking together*. New York: Currency.

Jacobs, E. D. (2000, August 31). *Performance audit: Idyllwild Charter High School.*

Kohn, A. (1993). *Punished by rewards: The trouble with gold stars, incentive plans, A's, praise, and other bribes.* New York: Houghton Mifflin.

Kohn, A. (1998). *What to look for in a classroom . . . and other essays.* San Francisco: Jossey-Bass.

Kohn, A. (2000). *The case against standardized testing.* Portsmouth, NH: Heinemann.

Kovalik, S., & Olsen, K. (1997) *Integrated thematic instruction: The model* (3rd ed.). Washington, DC: Books for Educators.

Lakoff, G. (1987). *Women, fire, and dangerous things: What categories reveal about the mind.* Chicago: University of Chicago Press.

Lakoff, G., & Johnson M. (1980). *Metaphors we live by.* Chicago: University of Chicago Press.

Land, G. (1986). *Grow or die: The unifying principle of transformation* (Rev. Ed.). Phoenix: Leadership 2000.

Langer, E. (1989). *Mindfulness.* Reading, MA: Addison-Wesley.

LeDoux, J. (1996). *The emotional brain.* New York: Simon & Schuster.

Lehman, N. (1999, September 6). Behind the SAT. *Newsweek, 52–57.*

Managuel, A. (1996). *A history of reading.* London: Flamingo.

Leonhardt, D., & Kerwin, K. (1997, June 30). Hey kid, buy this: Is Madison Avenue taking "get 'em while they're young" too far? *Business Week.*

MacLean, P. D. (1978). A mind of three minds: Educating the triune brain. In J. Shall & A. Minsky (eds.), *Education and the brain* (pp. 308–42). Chicago: University of Chicago Press.

McNeil, L. & Valenzuela, V. (2000). The harmful impact of the TAAS system of testing in Texas: Beneath the accountability rhetoric. G. Orfield & M. Koinhaber (eds.), prepared for *Raising standards or raising barriers? In equality and high-stakes testing in public education.* Harvard Civil Rights Project. From the World Wide Web: http://www.law.harvard.edu/civilrights/conferences.

Meier, D. (2000). *Will standards save public education?* Boston, MA: Beacon Press.

Norris, M. *ABC News.* 2/16/99.

Moustafa, M. & Land, R. (2000). *The research base of open court and its translation into instructional policy in California.* From the World Wide Web: http://curriculum.calstatela.edu/margaret.moustafa

O'Keefe, J., & Nadel, L. (1978). *The hippocampus as a cognitive map.* Oxford: Clarendon Press.

Palmer, P. J. (1999). The grace of great things: Reclaiming the sacred in knowing, teaching and learning. In S. Glazer (ed.), *The heart of learning*. New York: Jeremy Tarcher/Putnam.

Parasuraman, R. (ed.) (1998). *The attentive brain*. Cambridge, MA: MIT Press.

Partnership School Design, (1994). New York: The Edison Project.

Peat, F. David. (1996). *Blackfoot physics: A journey into the Native American universe*. London: Fourth Estate.

Perkins, D. (1995). *Outsmarting IQ: The emerging science of learnable intelligence*. New York: Free Press.

Perry, B., Pollard, R. A., Baker, W. L., & Vigilaute, D. (1955, Winter). Childhood trauma, the neurobiology of adaptation, and use-dependent development of the brain: How states become traits. *Infant Mental Health Journal*.

Pert, C. B. (1997). *Molecules of emotion*. New York: Scribner.

The Proof. (1997). NOVA. Videotape. WGBH Boston.

Portner, J. (2000, December 6). Pressure to pass tests permeates Virginia classrooms. *Education Week, xx*(14), 1, 20.

Restak, R. (1995). *Brainscapes*. New York: Hyperion.

Sapolsky, R. M. (1998). *Why zebras don't get ulcers*. New York: W. H. Freeman.

Sarason, S. B. (1990). *The predictable failure of educational reform: Can we change course before it's too late?* San Francisco: Jossey-Bass.

Schacter, D. (1996). *Searching for memory: The brain, the mind, and the past*. New York: Basic Books.

Schon, D. A. (1983). *The reflective practioner.* New York: Basic Books.

Schopenhauer, A. (1966). *The world as will and representation (Die Welt als Wille und Vorstellung)*. (E. F. J. Payne, English trans.). New York: Dover Publications.

Siegel, D. J. (1999). *The developing mind: Towards neurobiology of interpersonal experience*. New York: The Guilford Press.

Senge, P. M. (1990). *The fifth discipline: The art and practice of the learning organization*. New York: Doubleday.

Schmahmann, J. D. (Ed.). (1997). The cerebellum and cognition. *International Review of Neurobiology* (Vol. 41). San Diego: Academic Press.

Sizer, T. R. (1997). *Horace's school: Redesigning the American high school*. Boston: Houghton Mifflin.

Squire, L. R., & Kandel, E. R. (1999). *Memory: From mind to molecules*. New York: W. H. Freeman.

Swanson, J. *et. al.* (1998). Attention-deficit/hyperactivity disorder: Symptom domains, cognitive processes, and neural networks. In R. Parasuraman, (Ed.) *The Attentive Brain* (pp. 445–60). Cambridge: MIT Press.

Vaill, P. B. (1996). *Learning as a way of being.* San Francisco: Jossey-Bass.

Vygotsky, L. S. (1978). *Mind in society.* Cambridge: Harvard University Press.

Walsh, M. (1999, November 24). Ka-Ching! Business cashing in on learning. *Education Week, XIX*(13), 10, 13–16.

Weiner, J. (1999). *Time, love, memory: A great biologist and his quest for the origins of behavior.* New York: Alfred A. Knopf.

Wentworth, P. (1950). *Through the Wall.* New York: Harper & Row.

Wenger, E. (1999). *Communities of practice: Learning, meaning and identity.* New York: Cambridge University Press.

Wheatley, M. (1999). *Leadership and the new science: Discovering order in a chaotic world* (2nd ed.). San Francisco: Berrett-Koehler.

Wheatley, M. & Kellner-Rogers, M. (1998). *A simpler way.* San Francisco: Berrett-Koehler.

Whitehead, A. N. (1978). Process and reality. D. R. Griffin & D. W. Sherbusne. New York: Free Press.

Woolfolk, A. E. (1993). *Educational psychology* (5th ed.). Boston: Allyn and Bacon.

Yeats, W. B. (1922). The second coming. In R. J. Finneran. *The Collected Poems of W. B. Yeats* (1996) (2nd rev. ed.). New York: Scribner.

Zajonc, A. (1993). *Catching the light: What is light and how so we see it?* New York: Oxford University Press.

NEWSPAPER ARTICLES

Berliner, D. C. (2001, January 28). Our schools versus theirs: Averages that hide the true extremes. *Washington Post,* p. B03.

Brady, E. (1999, August 25). *USA Today,* p. 08C.

Colvin, R. L. (1999, November 18). *Los Angeles Times,* p. A-3.

Fiore, F., & Simon, R. (2000, September 14). Hollywood acknowledge kids exposure to violence. *Los Angeles Times.*

Gabler, N. (2000, March 12). How little we know: The trip from knowledge to "knowingness." *Los Angeles Times,* p. M-1.

Henderson, A. (2000, April 20). *The Sydney Morning Herald,* p. 19.

Lesher, D. (1999, January 7). Budget tight, schools come first, Davis says. *Los Angeles Times,* p. A-1.

Magnier, M. (2001, February 9). Japan wants its students to learn—for the joy of it. *Los Angeles Times,* p. A5.

Norwood, R. (2000, October 3). USA basketball tired of this kind of dream. *Los Angeles Times*, D8.

Schrage, M. (1989, December 8). America's sense of design finally starting to take shape. *Los Angeles Times*, p. D1.

Shedden. M. (1999, March 5). Pillow hoisting robots to compete. *Florida Today.*

Third home-taught youth off to Harvard. (1987, December 31). *Los Angeles Times*, p. 21.

Story on Doug Flutie (1999, August 25). *USA Today*, p. 8c.

The Weekend Australian, (2000, April 22–23), p. 27.

Helf, D. (1999, August 22). Sacramento gets high marks in school reform. *Los Angeles Times*, p. A1.

REPORTS AND STUDIES

A Nation at Risk, 1983 The Imperative for Educational Reform. A Report to the Nation and the Secretary of Education United States Department of Education by The National Commission on Excellence in Education April 1983.

A Nation Still At Risk. An Education Manifesto. April 30, 1998. The Center for Education Reform. (edreform.com).

elearning: Putting a World-class Education at the Finger tips of All Children. U.S. Department of Education. December 15, 2000.

Goals 2000: Educate America Act (P.L. 103–227).

Issues Related to Estimating the Home Schooled Population in the United States, National Center of Education Statistics. Technical Report, Sept. 2000.

Kids & Media @ the new millennium: A comprehensive national analysis of children's media use. (November, 1999). The Henry J. Kaiser Family Foundation. www.kff.org.

NAEP 1999 Trends in Academic Progress: Three Decades of Student Performance, NCES 2000-469, by J. R. Campbell, C. M. Hombo, & J. Mazzeo. Washington, DC: 2000. U.S. Department of Education. Office of Educational Research and Improvement. National Center for Education Statistics.

Student Performance Report Executive Summary, 1999–2000. Texas Education Agency, Student Assessment Division. (www.tea.state.tx.us/student.assessment)

The Third International Mathematics and Science Study (TIMSS) nces.ed.gov/timss/timss95/index.asp

Third International Mathematics and Science Study (TIMSS-R). Web release, December 5, 2000. (nces.ed.gov/pubsearch)

Grissmer, D., A. Flanagan, J. Kawata & S. Williamson. (2000). *Improving Student Achievement: What NAEP Test Scores Us.* Santa Monica: RAND.

Klein, S. P., L. Hamilton, D. McCaffrey & B. M. Stecher. (2000). *What do Test Scores in Texas Tell Us?* Santa Monica: RAND.

WEB SITES

www.bced.gov.bc.ca/irp/

www.chembio.uoguelph.ca/educmat/chm386/rudiment/tourquan/broglie.htm

www.Cainelearning.com

www.creatinglearningcommunities.org

www.curriculum.calstatela.edu/faculty/margaret.moustafa

www.ed.gov/G2K/

www.edreform.com

www.gatesfoundation.org

www.Gossamerridge.com

www.kff.org

www.law.harvard.edu/civilrights/conferences

www.nces.ed.gov/timss/timss95/index.asp

www.nces.ed.gov/pubsearch

www.sacsa.sa.edu

www.Suzukiassociation.org

www.tahatai.school.nz

www.tea.state.tx.us/student.assessment

www.thelearningweb.net

www.usfirst.org

About the Authors

Geoffrey and Renate Caine are pioneers in synthesizing neuroscience with research from other fields in a way that is of practical value to those interested in education. They are writers and educational consultants and work throughout the United States, Canada, Europe, Australia, and New Zealand.

Geoffrey has been a lecturer in law at the University of N.S.W. in Australia, education services manager of a software company, and national director of the Mind/Brain Network of the American Society for Training and Development.

Renate is professor emerita of education at California State University, San Bernardino, where she was also director of the Center for Integrative Learning and Teaching. She was an award-winning teacher and has taught or researched every level of education—from kindergarten to college.

The Caines have published extensively. Their first book, *Making Connections: Teaching and the Human Brain* (ASCD, 1991; Addison Wesley Longman, 1994), has had a distribution of over 200,000 copies. Other books include: *Education on the Edge of Possibility*, which describes their work with two schools over a five-year period and deals with the systems changes facing education; and *Unleashing the Power of Perceptual Change: The Promise of Brain Based Learning* (ASCD, 1997), which describes the nature of the personal and professional development necessary for teaching in an age of information, technology, and uncertainty.

The Caines's work can be found in state, district and school curricula, and in instructional and staff development materials such as the California Secondary Task Force Report "Second to None," and they have been featured on *Teacher TV*, Discovery Channel, and *Future Quest,* PBS.

They can be contacted through their Web site, www.Cainelearning. com.